# About the Author

Angela Chaney has been a writer and marketer since 2000. She has worked as an editor-in-chief for a business magazine and has written articles and marketing pieces for hundreds of different industries.

She is also a fiction writer who has published a cozy mystery book and is always working on some piece of fiction.

Angela is currently the co-owner of Pixel Fire Marketing. She heads up the company's content department and writes blog posts, website content, articles and social media posts as well as focusing on marketing strategy for the company's clients and internal campaigns.

@ANGELAWOLTMAN

Angela Woltman

# Contents

# Introduction

## What is
## Engagement Equity?

# What is Engagement Equity?

I've spent my entire career in sales, so the concept of *providing value* has been hammered into my brain for more than 18 years. As a print ad salesperson and editor for a local business magazine, I naturally provided *value* in the form of feature articles and press releases, but always felt uncomfortable with the framework of our organization, which required clients to purchase ad space before we'd include them in our content.

I couldn't put into words why this *pay-to-play* as I heard it called many times made me uneasy, but I knew that it just wasn't the right way to do business.

What I didn't realize is that I knew, deep down, that instead of building equity with our potential clients before we asked them for an ad buy, we were in fact doing the opposite: we were asking for something (an ad buy) that we had not earned the right to ask for (by building equity).

## JOINING PIXEL FIRE MARKETING

I left the magazine and started my own business, still in the marketing field, and my partners and I began our quest for what we would be known for.

My business partner had a heavy SEO background and had started to dip his toes into the Social Media Management field, so we gravitated toward these avenues and soon added website development to our repertoire. As I got deeper and deeper into the social media world I started to feel the same uneasiness that I'd felt at the magazine.

Almost all of the businesses I knew that were on social media were selling something.

*"Check out our happy hour! Come to our open house! Look at our new products!"*

It just didn't seem right and it didn't make me want to give them business.

## WAS I THE ONLY ONE?

I wasn't. I am not. As I did more research and started to follow educated and savvy marketers such as Gary Vaynerchuk, I realized that I was feeling this way for a reason. **These businesses were doing it WRONG.** Instead of providing value to their followers through great content, they were instead pushing themselves onto people who just wanted to scroll through their feeds for some funny videos or to see what their friends were up to.

5

## SO WHAT TO DO?

The solution, which we adopted at the core of our social media process, was to encourage our clients to aspire to the 80/20 rule.

80% of what they post should **not be about them at all** and should provide value in the form of being entertaining, useful, or informative. This then gave them the right to use the remaining 20% of their posts for *the ask*.

*Think of the 80% as priming the pump and gearing up for the 20%, which is the sell.*

I can't tell you how many times I have told people about the 80/20 rule. Most of the time, the person sitting across from me seems to get it. They nod their head and say it makes sense and often times, I think I've inspired a light bulb moment.

But invariably, these same people would go right back to posting their open houses or they'd ask why in the world we were posting information that *"did not apply to them at all"* on their Facebook pages.

Then one morning, as I was taking a walk, I listened to a podcast on marketing. And while it wasn't really saying anything that I hadn't previously known, the way it was STATED affected me in a much different way. Thinking of the 80/20 rule in terms of earning a person's respect and loyalty resonated with me and I knew that it would resonate with our clients as well.

## 80/20 RULE: EARNING RESPECT & LOYALTY

Of course, my brain didn't just say, "Great, good way to change the way I talk about this to my clients! Moving on." Nope. My brain doesn't work that way. When I hear something that inspires me, my brain goes CRAZY.

So I kept thinking and turning over the concept in my mind. *How do we put our own spin on this concept and make it ours?*

**80**

**INFORMATIVE
ENTERTAINING
USEFUL**

**20**

**PROMOTE
SELL**

## THE CORE OF OUR BUSINESS

So I went back to the core of our business. What were we really trying to push through every single thing we sold? **Engagement.**

We were always pushing for more engagement. And then it clicked. **Engagement Equity.**

## MAKING DEPOSITS

Were our clients depositing enough into their engagement accounts to earn the right to ask their prospects for anything?

I presented this to our team the next day and I could just see their eyes light up. This was a different way of presenting our core values and beliefs in a language that people understood.

Being the content writer that I am, I next wrote up a blog post to spell out the concept. In the first draft, I said that "we are all doing this (building equity) subconsciously every day with our friends, family and business colleagues."

Hmmm.

As I went to edit the post before I published it, I got stuck on that sentence. And I changed it. It became "we are all HOPEFULLY doing this subconsciously every day with our friends, family and business colleagues."

And I published it.

## FRAME OF MIND

But I couldn't stop thinking about it. Are most of us REALLY doing this? Are we focused on depositing into our equity accounts before we ask for anything in our personal lives? With our employees? In networking groups?

Or are we instead stuck in the "I did this for Albert and Albert hasn't reciprocated" mindset? Or, even worse, the "What have you done for me lately?" frame of mind?

I was guilty of it myself. As a recent transplant to a new city and being in that 'making new friends' mode, I'd often found myself inviting a potential new gal pal out for a glass of wine and wondering why they either scheduled it out so far into the future that we both forgot, or didn't respond at all. *Did no one like me??*

Similarly, I'd also gone to a new networking group and got up week after week to talk about our awesome new web packages and wondered, week after week, why no one was asking to learn more about them.

Looking back on these personal instances, it occurred to me: I'm not using the Engagement Equity (EE) theory in hardly any part of my life!

And if I'm not, it's likely that a bunch of other people aren't either.

*Engagement Equity Model*

# Inviting Out a New Friend

### SCENARIO #1

I ask a new potential friend out for a glass of wine and think, "Well, I invited her to do something, why didn't she jump at the chance?" In the best case scenario, I deposited once into our equity account by giving her the chance to drink wine with my spectacular self (self-deprecating joke alert), then expected an immediate return on investment by her accepting.

> "Well, I invited her to do something, why didn't she jump at the chance?"

In the most likely scenario, I withdrew from our account without ever putting anything in because I asked her to do something (have a glass of wine with me when it's very possible she would have rather been shopping with her real friends or taking out the trash for all we know.) Yeah, when you look at it like that, it's no wonder the poor chick never scheduled our get-together.

### SCENARIO #1 RE-IMAGINED

I meet a potential new friend at a networking event. Before we leave the event, I make sure to ask her about her family and hobbies and really listen to her reply. DEPOSIT

A few days later, I'm talking to an acquaintance who I think would make a good client for said possible new bud and so I connect the two of them. DEPOSIT

A few days after that, I connect with her on social media and leave a nice comment on one of the pictures she posts of her daughter. DEPOSIT *Then I proceed with the invitation.*

I think we all know that the result would be very different. And guess what? It was. Just like a sales prospect or a connection on social media, relationship-building takes time. After making a few deposits into our new friendship account, this new friend was happy to have a glass of wine with me and that delightful conversation not only sparked a new friendship, but also allowed me to learn more about her so I could continue to make meaningful deposits into our relationship account.

# Creating Referrals in a Networking Group

## SCENARIO #2

I join a new networking group and make everyone listen to me talk about my business week after week (every time a withdrawal). I try to listen as all the other members talk about their businesses, but I never really follow up or do much about it (no deposits there!). I get really excited about our new web packages and can't wait to present them, especially because there are two or three members in the group whom I know can really benefit from them.

I get up and talk and... crickets. But can't they see what value I am providing for them?? Nope. All I've done is once again ask them for something. I'm trying to make a withdrawal on an account that I've made zero deposits in.

## SCENARIO #2 RE-IMAGINED

I join a new networking group and introduce myself, but don't go much into our products or services. Instead, I listen carefully to all of the members and pick out two whom I think would be good people for me to connect with. I schedule one-to-ones with them and really listen to who they are, what they do, and what would help them out. Deposit

I find a couple of people in my network who I think would be a good fit for them and connect them via email. DEPOSIT

At the next meeting, I get up and talk about how great it was getting to know them and how happy my colleagues were to be connected to such great business people. DEPOSIT

I then find an interesting article or book recommendation for each of them based on their unique businesses or hobbies and email them a link. DEPOSIT

## THE IMPACT OF ENGAGEMENT EQUITY

What do you think is going to happen NOW when I present those new web packages?

I'll tell you what happened. One of the above mentioned group members asked to hear more about them and the other one gave me a referral for one of their clients who might be interested.

## WOW. THIS. STUFF. WORKS.

The Engagement Equity idea might have sprung from the social media world, but it really applies to every single facet of our lives.

We can't wait to explain more about how this all works and how YOU can apply it today in your business, with your family, in your community, and of course, on your social media networks.

*Ready to go on the Engagement Equity journey with us? We promise you it will change your life.*

# Part One

## Engagement Equity in Business

# CHAPTER ONE

# Engagement Equity in Social Media

## ENGAGEMENT EQUITY IN SOCIAL MEDIA

It makes sense that we'd start this book in the area where it all started: social media. Even though I now believe that Engagement Equity is a way of life and that it can enhance any part of your life, we need to start somewhere, right?

One of the biggest influencers in the social media realm (and the person I learned my personal business theories from) is Gary Vaynerchuck, more commonly known as Gary Vee. An immigrant who has made a huge name for himself through pure hustle and innovative thinking, Gary Vee has books you can read, a website you can peruse, podcasts you can listen to, social media accounts you can follow... you get the idea.

*Gary Vaynerchuk*

**12 MILLION FOLLOWERS**   **5x NEW YORK TIMES BEST SELLING AUTHOR**   **$160 MILLION NET WORTH**

This guy gets more done in his business by 5pm on Monday than most of us accomplish in a month. Though you can easily get exhausted by listening to this freak of nature (I say that in the nicest possible way), you can also stand to learn a ton.

Although Gary Vee's material tends to get outdated quickly as he is always talking about the cutting edge in new apps and platforms, the underlying theme to everything he says can be summed up in a quote from one of his first books, *The Thank You Economy*.

## OUTCARE THEM

I mean, it's fantastic! But how many business owners actually think this way? And, more importantly for our topic of discussion, how many of them show they think that way through their social media?

**What many of us have forgotten is that social media is meant to be social.**

That's how it was designed, that's what it was intended for and that's how people respond best to it.

Somewhere along the way, though, business owners turned it into a selling tool. Instead of reaching out and interacting and engaging, they treated it like they would a radio or television ad and just used it to blare out their message.

## WHAT DOES SOCIAL REALLY MEAN?

To me social is synonymous with sharing. To be social with friends, you share a meal or a round of drinks or great conversation. To be social with acquaintances, you share what you think of the seminar you're in or what you thought of *The Bachelorette* last night.

To be social with your employees, you arrange an after-work bowling outing or happy hour so you can all get to know each other better.

What's the common theme here? Being social and sharing is a two-way street. You both give, therefore you are both (hopefully) enriched by the experience.

When you're blaring out your message on social media, you undercut what the entire experience is supposed to be about. You make it a one-way street, then wonder why no one is responding.

## HOW TO CREATE A SOCIAL COMMUNITY

You share with them, of course. And every time you share with them, as long as it's some quality sharing, you're making a deposit in your Engagement Equity account and you're showing them you care about them.

## SHARE WITH YOUR COMMUNITY

By sharing, in this instance, we are not talking about that little 'share' button you see on every Facebook post.

Although sharing your community's posts can sometimes be a very good idea, what we're talking about here is sharing a bit of yourself.

This can come in the form of your expertise (sharing a tip or trick of the industry), your sense of humor (we all know funny jokes, photos and videos do extremely well on social media) or even just some of your story.

When you reach out to your social community in this way, you're showing them that you're interested in building a relationship and that you're willing to offer up some great value to get that relationship established.

To put it in our terms, you're demonstrating that you're ready to start making some deposits into that Engagement Equity account because you care about them and want to build a relationship.

# What We See Most Often on a Bar's Social Media Account

In the bar owner's mind, he probably think he's giving some value right?

After all, he's offering some discounts on drinks for happy hour, has created this great new mixed drink that he thinks is delicious, and is bringing in a cool new act to entertain his clientele! Give, give, give!

## WHY THIS DOESN'T WORK

What he's actually doing is ask, ask, ask. Why? Because he's selling.

He's asking people to come spend their hard-earned dollars at his bar by buying happy hour drinks, ordering his new cocktail, and spending a few hours (and dollars) at his establishment on a Saturday night.

**He's withdrawing from an equity account that he's made no deposits into.**

| TRANSACTIONS |
| :---: |
| *Posted asking to try menu item* |
| WITHDRAWAL |
| *Posted asking to attend happy hour* |
| WITHDRAWAL |
| *Posted asking to come in* |
| WITHDRAWAL |

These are three engaging posts where the restaurant's followers are actually learning something. Then, who knows? Maybe they'll feel like trying out one of those martinis they were just learning about, or perhaps they'll get a hankerin' for an IPA after a nice juicy burger.

Even if they don't, they'll be primed to follow up and respond favorably to the next 'ask' that you do.

**Of course, don't make the mistake of going in the opposite direction and never having an ask!**

We've seen this happen as well. If you keep putting out content and keep making deposits into that account, you earn the ask.

And if you don't do it? Not only will you not give your audience a chance to reciprocate, but you might also make them a little uncomfortable.

## OVERDOING THE DEPOSITS

Did you ever have one of those desperate friends who was willing to do anything for you? They would have driven through the night in a hailstorm to pick you up from the airport, bring you cookies at work if you had a craving, and watch your dog while you took that two-week cruise to the West Indies and never asked for anything in return.

Did you appreciate this friend?

Or did you start to get a little uneasy and wonder what was wrong with them?

More than likely, you ended up thinking they were a little pathetic and eased yourself away from them.

## IT'S THE SAME THING WITH MARKETING

If you've put in enough equity, you've earned that ask. When you don't do it, it's like saying you don't have enough confidence in your business or your marketing skills to make the request. And who wants to do business with someone who has no confidence in their own product?

Once you establish a good pattern of giving and asking (or giving, giving, giving, and asking), you'll steadily gain an audience who checks your social media often and begins engaging with it by sharing and commenting. And, as we all know, the more your followers like, share and comment, the more they'll see your posts (and the less you'll have to spend on boosts or ads).

But the biggest gain of all is that you're building an *engaged* audience, which lets you put into action the next stage of Gary Vee's 'outcaring' campaign. When your audience knows they can continually get great content when they engage with your page, they'll start to trust you. **And when they trust you, they'll talk to you.**

## TALK WITH YOUR AUDIENCE

This is where the golden opportunity is with social media. Once your audience begins 'talking' to you (by tweeting at you, tagging you in posts or sharing pictures of

your establishment or products), you can talk back. You should never let a tweet go un re-tweeted (yes, we're coining that new term), never let a mention go by without a comment and, believe it or not, never let a negative post or review transpire without responding to it.

As Gary Vee so wonderfully explains in his book, the social media world has allowed consumers to go back to the olden days when they expected excellent one-to-one customer service.

Gone are the days when bad service got swept under the rug because a slighted customer had no one to tell except their friends and family. With the invention of social media, they can blast it out to the world, and they expect a response from YOU, the business owner.

Yes, it sounds frightening. But wouldn't you much rather know that you have an unhappy customer out there and be given a chance to right that wrong? No matter what type of negative comment you see (whether deserved or not, whether even TRUE or not), respond to it. Even if it's just a, "We're so sorry this happened to you, please give us your contact information so we can find out how to make it right," you're showing the customer *and everyone else who sees the response* that you care.

And every time you show that you care, you are making a deposit into the Engagement Equity account of a number of current and potential customers.

# *Engagement Equity in Social Media*

| MONDAY | TUESDAY | WEDNESDAY | THURSDAY | FRIDAY | SATURDAY | SUNDAY |
|---|---|---|---|---|---|---|
| **WEEK ONE** | | | | | | |
| local industry article<br>DEPOSIT | | how-to video<br>DEPOSIT | invitation to open house<br>**boost this!**<br>WITHDRAWAL | community event<br>DEPOSIT | | shout-out to local business<br>DEPOSIT |
| **WEEK TWO** | | | | | | |
| | DIY project or recipe<br>DEPOSIT | special offer for a product<br>WITHDRAWAL | | listing of networking events coming up<br>DEPOSIT | | |

**Use the blank template on the next page to follow along.**

## SOCIAL MEDIA CHALLENGE

Create a 2-week social calendar for your business that balances 3–4 engaging posts (DEPOSIT) to every one promotional post (WITHDRAWAL). Aim for 4–5 posts each week, so that your calendar will look something like this:

### WEEK ONE

**Monday:** Local article on the industry you're a part of  DEPOSIT

**Wednesday:** How-to or funny video  DEPOSIT

**Thursday:** Invitation to your weekend open house  WITHDRAWAL

**Friday:** Upcoming local community event  DEPOSIT

**Sunday:** Shout-out to local business you frequent  DEPOSIT

### WEEK TWO

**Tuesday:** DIY project or recipe  DEPOSIT

**Wednesday:** Special offer for one of your products or services  WITHDRAWAL

**Thursday:** Recommendation of a great new restaurant in town  DEPOSIT

**Friday:** Listing of networking events coming up in the next couple of weeks  DEPOSIT

At the end of your two-week period, evaluate which posts got the most likes, shares, comments, re-tweets, favorites, etc. When you create your next two-week calendar, include more of the types of posts that got the most engagement.

# Weekly Social Media Calendar

| DATE | BODY COPY | PHOTO | LINK | NOTES |
|------|-----------|-------|------|-------|
|      |           |       |      |       |
|      |           |       |      |       |
|      |           |       |      |       |
|      |           |       |      |       |
|      |           |       |      |       |
|      |           |       |      |       |

# CHAPTER TWO

# Engagement Equity in Networking

## BUILDING EQUITY IN NETWORKING

Ah, networking. Some of us see it as a necessary evil and dread every time we need to attend a new group.

Others thrive on the prospect of rubbing elbows with potential clients on a regular basis and dislike the times they must be chained to their desk and NOT out and about with other business people.

No matter which camp you fall into, networking has become a necessity in nearly every industry. Even though it seems you can find out almost anything about anyone these days just by firing up your computer and doing a few simple searches, most people still choose to do business with those they know, like and trust. **And what is STILL the best way to get to know, like and trust someone?** *In person.*

Yes, you can back up your reputation with a great website and a solid social media strategy (and we absolutely recommend that), but if you are trying to do business in your geographic area, you still have to show up and shake a few hands.

"

The currency of real networking is not greed, but generosity.

**KEITH FERRAZZI**

# How Much Do You Need to Give in Order to Gain?

**For the purpose of this book, we'll split up networking groups into two types: Recurring and Random.**

Recurring are the groups that meet on a weekly, bi-weekly or monthly basis while random groups are those that may only meet one time or that attract different businesspeople each time they get together.

Why are we splitting them up? Well, it's just like Texas Hold'em, where your strategy is different depending on whether you're playing in a tournament or a limit cash game (have I mentioned I love poker?).

Your strategy for Engagement Equity in a networking group is going to depend on whether you get the opportunity to see the same people over and over on a regular basis or whether you've got to find a way to keep making deposits in their account when they only encounter you once.

## RECURRING NETWORKING GROUPS

A recurring group is one that meets on a regular basis, usually weekly. These groups have the same people involved as members, though guests sometimes attend.

Those of us at my marketing company have been involved in recurring networking groups for many years, so we've seen what works—and what doesn't. However, a lot of members just don't seem to understand what it takes to get referrals or leads and a lot of them get frustrated.

Inevitably, they end up wondering: *How MUCH do you need to give in order to gain?*

The least successful members of our groups saw it as a 'tit for tat' type of arrangement. If I give a referral to John, then John should in turn give a referral to me. And if he didn't? Well, John obviously wasn't doing what he was supposed to, so I'm never giving a referral to John again!

# What's Wrong With This Situation?

**Well, the 'tit for tat' model of business (or living, for that matter), just doesn't work. Why? There are a number of reasons, including:**

## THE OTHER PERSON MAY NOT BE IN A POSITION TO GIVE BACK RIGHT NOW.

So you gave a referral to John, who is a plumber, to come and fix your backed up toilet. Your profession is home real estate. It's pretty presumptuous to think that John has a whole host of people who want to buy homes in his back pocket. In fact, it could be months before John runs across someone who is looking to buy or sell. It doesn't mean he's violating the Givers Gain code of conduct: he just has no referrals to give.

## THEY WANT TO MAKE SURE THEY CAN TRUST YOU.

Most people are pretty careful about putting their name and reputation on the line to recommend another business. This is especially true if that person is in a sensitive profession where trust is essential (like a financial planner or in healthcare).

Although John, as a plumber, may not be in one of those professions, it's likely that he's built his small plumbing business by getting homeowners to trust his services and his reputation, and John is likely very protective of that. Just because you gave him a referral doesn't mean you've earned his trust. You've started on the path, but everyone's trust path is different.

## THEY MIGHT BE BUSY GIVING TO SOMEONE ELSE.

John very well could have given until he was blue in the face all month in the networking group—he just wasn't giving to YOU. The whole point of the recurring networking model is that everyone is giving to everyone else in the group, it will all come back around to benefit them in the end.

Unfortunately, many members of networking groups don't get the bigger picture. If they're giving to a certain member and not seeing anything come back their way from that same member, they start to get angry.

# THE PRESSURE OF OBLIGATION IS UNCOMFORTABLE WHEN YOU CAN'T ACT ON IT.

**There's a reason why recurring networking groups rely on reciprocation to make their groups work: it creates an obligation.**

If you've studied the psychology of sales at all (or attended a sales training), you'll know that one of the key components is that by creating a sense of obligation with your prospect, you'll increase your chances of making a sale.

That's why sales people give away free product or bring in donuts and coffee when they meet with you. They've done you a favor, so it's more likely you'll do a favor (buy something from them) in return. When we give a referral, we've created a sense of obligation in the person who received the referral.

This, in turn, should make it much more likely that they will give you a referral in return.

**But what happens if one of the other reasons for NOT giving a referral mentioned above (or a different reason) is present?**

Now the person given the referral feels a sense of obligation to give back to you... but for some reason they can't.

How do you think that makes them feel? *Uncomfortable.*

And if that feeling persists, they might start avoiding you and eventually leave the group altogether because they feel they couldn't live up to that obligation.

# How is Engagement Equity Different Than the Practices We See in a Lot of Networking Groups?

## ENGAGEMENT EQUITY IS DIFFERENT

The big difference is that you're taking out that second part of the networking philosophy: If I give to others they will in turn give to me. With Engagement Equity, you're focused on making deposits. The goal is giving enough *so that you earn the right to ask for something in return*. You're not *expecting* someone to give you business simply because you gave them business. You're earning the right to even ask for it in the first place.

Remember our example of John the Plumber and the referral he got from you, the real estate agent?

**Let's see how this situation might play out if you were focused on Engagement Equity.**

You give John the Plumber a referral of one of your clients who just bought a home and is having trouble with the basement flooding. DEPOSIT

John does a good job, so you stand up in the group the next week and give a glowing testimonial on how happy your client was with John's work. DEPOSIT

You have some extra tickets to a baseball game that your real estate team has purchased, so you offer them to members of your group. You make a point of asking John personally after the meeting because you know he's a big baseball fan. DEPOSIT

You're having an open house for your team and one of the focuses is to bring in those in the home services industry who may be in a position to refer business to you. You ask John if he can attend and if he might know of an electrician he's done business with who would like to join him. WITHDRAWAL

You see the difference here? In the traditional networking model, you give a referral and then sit back and wait for a referral to be given to you in return. When that doesn't happen, you start to get bitter and you wonder if you should ever give John a referral again.

In the Engagement Equity model, you *make deposits* into the account in a number of different ways until you feel you've earned the right to *ask for something*. It's possible that even the three deposits into John's equity account could have resulted in zero if you hadn't followed it up with an ask that was easy for John to comply with.

You weren't asking for someone who wanted to sell their home (which is a pretty big ask), you were simply implying, "Hey, I've given you a lot of value over the past few weeks and now I'm just asking you to come pop into my open house for a half hour."

> ## "I've given you enough that I feel I've earned the right to ask."

It's the exact same way that Engagement Equity works in social media (though on a larger scale).

After making 3–4 deposits of engaging articles or event announcements or cute videos, you're then saying to your followers, "I've given you enough that I feel I've earned the right to ask you to click over to our website and look around a little to learn more about our company."

## RANDOM NETWORKING GROUPS

It's easy to put Engagement Equity into effect when you get the chance to be around the same people on a regular basis. You can even make schedules of how you're going to make deposits with certain members of the group and when because you know exactly when and how much you'll be seeing them over the course of the next few months.

It becomes more difficult when you're trying to build equity with those you see at random intervals. A good example of this would be a Chamber of Commerce.

The Chambers in our city range in size from a few hundred members to thousands, and you never know which of those people show up to what events or if they come to anything at all.

It's likely you'll start to get a feel for the core group that always come to ribbon cuttings or networking coffees, but there's still no guarantee that if Susan came to the happy hour last month, she'll be there again this month (or ever again, for that matter).

Though you'll need to do a bit more work in these types of situations, you can still make deposits and build relationships.

## START THE RELATIONSHIP OUT RIGHT

The key is to identify a few people at each event that you think would make good contacts for you and get their information.

Make sure you start the relationships out right by engaging with them at the event and really listening to who they are, what they do, and what makes them unique in their industry.

Follow this up with a call or email within the next couple of days asking them to have coffee with you and then find out how you can help them with their business.

This is pretty much a neutral act (not a deposit or a withdrawal) because you're asking them to do something (meet with you), but you're giving value in return by learning more about them.

It's also a necessary step in the process of relationship building.

Once you know more about them, you can start making deposits in the form of connections with others they might benefit from knowing, referrals, invitations to events they might like attending, etc. etc.

Make a few deposits, then figure out your ask. Maybe you'd like to meet their manager, who is in charge of decision-making for the company, or perhaps you know they're close with a prospect of yours and might be willing to arrange lunch for all of you.

> "A crowd has the collective wisdom of individual ignorance.

**THOMAS CARLYLE**

## INDIVIDUAL AND COLLECTIVE

As we build our businesses and our networks, it's important to look at our equity accounts in two different ways: **individual and collective**.

On an individual level, we have an equity account with John in our weekly networking group and we need to make sure we are depositing enough to ask for that withdrawal when the time comes.

However, we also need to look at our network *collectively*.

When you are putting helpful, free worksheets to download on your website, when you're sharing upcoming events on your Facebook page, when you're speaking at conferences and sharing your secrets to success, when you're connecting people... you're making deposits into the collective account.

You're not sure *who* they are specifically benefiting and therefore, you won't be sure *who*, exactly, you're earning the right to approach with an ask. But this doesn't make it any less important to make deposits.

The more deposits we make into collective accounts, the more we are establishing ourselves as a good person to know, trust, and eventually do business with.

And there also may come times (perhaps many times), when you need to make a collective ask.

*"Come to my seminar!"*

*"Visit my new website!"*

*"Read my new book!"*

The more you've deposited into that collective equity account, the better these requests will be received.

# Engagement Equity in Networking

**Use the blank template on the next page to complete this exercise.**

## NETWORKING EXERCISE

Make a list of your networking groups and split them into **recurring** and **random**.

For the **recurring groups**, write down all of the members you see on a regular basis. To start with, choose three you'd like to further your relationship with. Create a schedule to begin depositing into their equity account.

For the **random groups**, identify 3-4 people at the next function or get-together and collect their contact information. Then make the same schedule for them. For example:

## RECURRING NETWORKING GROUPS

- **MasterMind Group**
- **Referral Group**

## RANDOM NETWORKING GROUPS

- **Conference**
- **After Hours**

## RECURRING – ATTENDEES

**Robert Smith**

Deposit 1: *Like his business social media pages.*

Deposit 2: *Attend an event he is hosting.*

Deposit 3: *Refer a friend to him who is in need of his services.*

Withdrawal: Ask if he can introduce you to one of his LinkedIn connections.

**Cindy Winn**

Deposit 1: *Pass on a compliment you heard about her in another professional group.*

Deposit 2: *Comment on several of the posts she shares on her business Facebook page.*

Deposit 3: *Buy a product from her.*

Withdrawal: Invite her to attend a free informational seminar you are holding.

## RANDOM – ATTENDEES

**Trinity Keel – After Hours**

Deposit 1: *Compliment her on her dress and ask where she got it.*

Deposit 2: *Ask her why she got into the business she's in and really listen to the answer without interrupting.*

Deposit 3: *Ask her for an example of an ideal client.*

Withdrawal: Ask for her business card so you can keep in touch.

**Nicholas Staffer – Conference**

Deposit 1: *Sit by him at the conference and bring him a cup of coffee.*

Deposit 2: *Ask his opinion on one of the topics that is being discussed and closely listen to his answer.*

Deposit 3: *Offer to watch his coat and briefcase while he goes to get lunch.*

Withdrawal: Ask if you can have his contact info to schedule a lunch with him.

# Engagement Equity in Networking

## NETWORKING EXERCISE

Make a list of your networking groups and split them into **recurring** and **random**.

For the **recurring groups**, write down all of the members you see on a regular basis. To start with, choose three you'd like to further your relationship with. Create a schedule to begin depositing into their equity account.

For the **random groups**, identify 3-4 people at the next function or get-together and collect their contact information. Then make the same schedule for them.

### RECURRING NETWORKING GROUPS

- _____
- _____

### RANDOM NETWORKING GROUPS

- _____
- _____

### RECURRING – ATTENDEES

_____

Deposit 1:_____

Deposit 2:_____

Deposit 3:_____

Withdrawal:_____

_____

Deposit 1:_____

Deposit 2:_____

Deposit 3:_____

Withdrawal:_____

_____

Deposit 1:_____

Deposit 2:_____

Deposit 3:_____

Withdrawal:_____

### RANDOM – ATTENDEES

_____

Deposit 1:_____

Deposit 2:_____

Deposit 3:_____

Withdrawal:_____

_____

Deposit 1:_____

Deposit 2:_____

Deposit 3:_____

Withdrawal:_____

_____

Deposit 1:_____

Deposit 2:_____

Deposit 3:_____

Withdrawal:_____

# CHAPTER THREE

# Engagement Equity in The Office

## ENGAGEMENT EQUITY IN THE OFFICE

Being part of a team is HARD. Having been in work situations where I've been part of large teams as well as very small teams, I know that each team has its own struggles and that it's NEVER easy.

Teams full of women are no easier than co-ed teams. Teams heavy on leaders and light on employees struggle just as much as those that are headed up by one decision maker. I'm not sure if you're getting the gist here but... being a part of a team is hard, people!!

## TEAMS ALLOW US TO GET MORE STUFF DONE

Of course, what you can accomplish with a team is miles ahead of what you can do on your own, which is why most of us still make the choice to get a job in an office or start a company or join that committee instead of going it alone.

So our choice is NOT do I join a team or don't I? The choice becomes, do I do what it takes to succeed in a team environment and make it better or do I let the pressure take over and make me miserable?

I'm pretty sure all of us would choose to do what it takes to make things better (or at least I hope so.) However, no matter how much we may want to make things better, most of us just don't know how. And really, when you get down to it, it's no wonder why we're confused.

## PICTURING SUCCESS

When you picture a successful businessperson who is getting things done, making a lot of money and elevating the company to a new level, what do you see?

Do you see the ultra-polished executive who's willing to do whatever it takes to close that lead, make that sale and climb the next rung of the ladder?

Or do you see the empathetic team-player who is always doing his best to help out fellow team members, rarely taking credit for all the extra work he continually does?

## DOES SUCCESS = RUTHLESS?

Most people would choose the first example. It's been put in our heads that 'nice guys finish last,' especially when it comes to the world of business (and in dating, but that's another book altogether).

And so, we think that being 'successful' means being 'ruthless' and that if we really want to help others on the team be more successful, we're going to have to sacrifice something to do so.

So where does Engagement Equity come into this dog-eat-dog world?

Fortunately, according to organizational psychologist and author Adam Grant, it fits in perfectly. We just haven't been able to see it.

In his first book, *Give and Take*, Grant introduces the theory of three types of people in the workplace. There are your **Takers, Matchers,** and **Givers**.

"

Every time we interact with another person at work, we have a choice to make: do we try to claim as much value as we can, or contribute value without worrying about what we receive in return?"

**ADAM GRANT**

# How do Takers, Matchers and Givers Interact in the Workplace?

## TAKERS

Takers are the people we all probably think would be the most successful, but most of us can't bring ourselves to be this self-serving (thank goodness). They're the ones who ask others for help and then steal their ideas, who take credit for their colleagues' ideas, who will spread rumors if they think it will get a co-worker fired so they can get their position.

## MATCHERS

Matchers are the ones who say, "Okay, Sally stayed late and helped me with my proposal last week, so when she asks for my assistance on her sales pitch, I'm willing to put in a little extra work to help her out."

*Most of us are Matchers.* We're willing to help others if they help us, but we won't go that extra mile in most situations.

## GIVERS

The Givers are the ones who just seem to help out indiscriminately. Sally needs some help with her sales pitch? Well, Sally has never helped me out with anything but that's okay! I'm in a position to help and I will! They lend a hand wherever they can and to whomever they can. Givers give without ever asking for anything in return.

## WHO IS BEST IN THE WORKPLACE?

Now, in most people's opinion, the Matchers would probably be most successful at work. We all despise the Takers (and they tend to job hop as people figure out their true colors and do their best to get them ousted) and we think the Givers are doormats who never get ahead.

Of course, maybe most people think Matchers will be most successful because most of us ARE Matchers. What us Matchers might be surprised (and disappointed) to find out, though, is that Grant discovered that **the most successful people in the workplace were the Givers.**

## GIVERS SUCCESS IN THE WORKPLACE

The Givers built very loyal and deep connections within the workplace, from those they worked with to those they managed all the way up to those who ran the whole show. People were more willing to get on board with a Giver's vision because they honestly felt it would help the greater good and make the entire organization better.

There were exceptions, of course. The Givers who DID let themselves be taken advantage of by the Takers (which is bound to happen) tended to be less successful than the Givers who laid down some boundaries. But by and large, the Givers continually rise to the top.

## ENGAGEMENT EQUITY

How does this translate into Engagement Equity? That's a pretty easy one! **Givers were making deposits left, right, and center.** And the more deposits they made, the more their colleagues were willing to get on board, to help them out, to further their goals and visions. That's Engagement Equity in a nutshell.

While the Takers were withdrawing from an account with nothing in it (borrowing on equity credit, as you might call it) and Matchers were making a deposit only to pull it out as soon as they could, the Givers knew the value of building that account.

Building Engagement Equity in the office has its own list of challenges that don't exist in other areas, which can often make it a tough place to put the theory into practice. For one

thing, you're forced to be in an environment with a few (or a bunch) of people that you may or may not like or even get along with. Not only do you have to be in the same building (or sometimes even the same room) as these people, but you also have to find a way to create, sell, serve customers or do whatever else it is that your business does with these people. You don't just need to put up with co-workers: you have to find a way to make magic happen with these people every single day!

## MAKE TEAMWORK SIMPLE

And this brings us back to my initial statement in this chapter: being a part of a team is HARD. It can be so easy to get into the blame game or the '*I'm the only one working really hard*' gripe or to start questioning if everyone is contributing.

That's one of the beauties of Engagement Equity. All of the justifications and second-guessing stop. **You simply focus on giving more.**

*Ann didn't get her report done and asked for your help at the last minute?* **Give her the help.**

*Joe put in 1/10 of the work on the project and took 9/10th of the credit?* **Give him the credit.**

*You see a newbie who everyone thinks will be fired soon struggling with how to work the new operating system?* **Give him 20 minutes of your time and help out.**

It's really that easy. When you begin making deposits in your co-workers' accounts, it might take a while before you see the results. But believe me, you will see them.

# Part Two

## Engagement Equity in Relationships

# CHAPTER FOUR

# Engagement Equity in Romantic Relationships

## ENGAGEMENT EQUITY IN ROMANTIC RELATIONSHIPS

Remember when I said being part of a team is hard? Well, it's nothing compared to maintaining a healthy and loving relationship.

Ask anyone who has ever considered, been in, or ended a relationship (i.e. every single person on the planet), and they'll tell you the same thing. **Relationships are no walk in the park!**

Why are they so difficult? Well, there are a number of reasons, the largest of which is how important this person is in your life.

Your romantic partner SHOULD be your confidante, the one and only person whom you're walking this entire road you can call life with and, basically, the most important factor in your happiness and success.

Whoa.

When you put it like that, it sounds like A LOT of pressure. And it is. But when a relationship is healthy and supportive and loving, it's worth every single bit of effort you put into it.

And, what's more, being in a healthy relationship actually gives you the strength you need to go out and face the world every day.

> It turns out that the ability to step into the world on our own often stems from the knowledge that there is someone beside us whom we can count on—this is the 'dependency paradox'.

**AMIR LEVINE &
RACHEL HELLER**

## HEALTHY RELATIONSHIPS ARE KEY

In the fascinating book, *Attached. The New Science of Adult Attachment*, Amir Levine, M.D. and Rachel S.F. Heller, M.A. state:

> "It turns out that the ability to step into the world on our own often stems from the knowledge that there is someone beside us whom we can count on—this is the 'dependency paradox'. The logic of this paradox is hard to follow at first.
>
> How can we act more independent by being thoroughly dependent on someone else? If we had to describe the basic premise of adult attachment in one sentence, it would be: If you want to take the road to independence and happiness, find the right person to depend on and travel down it with that person."

**In other words, we are biologically programmed to need a partner to function at our prime level.**

Wow, that puts a different spin on things, huh? Needing someone to share our lives with is NOT bad—it's nature!

But back to why relationships are so difficult to find, nurture, and maintain. Although there are clearly enough reasons to write thousands of books on (and thousands upon thousands of books HAVE been written on this topic alone), one of the biggest challenges is that men and women are different.

I know it sounds obvious enough to be laughable. But even though most of us would agree with this broad statement, not many of us actually realize how differently men and women operate.

## WOMEN VS MEN

If you've never read *Men Are From Mars, Women are From Venus* by John Gray, Ph.D., I highly recommend it.

Actually, I more recommend the follow-up, *Mars and Venus, Together Forever* because it drops a lot of the hokey alien references and just gets down to the nitty gritty. In this book, the author points out a number of biological differences between our genders, including (but certainly not limited to):

- **Men need to feel important while women need to feel cherished.**
- **Women want to talk out their feelings while men just want to solve the problem.**
- **Men feel closest to someone when they are performing an activity side-by-side.**
- **Women feel close to someone when they are having conversations and sharing feelings.**
- **Women can go from one type of situation to another without the need for downtime.**
- **Men often need time to decompress after a day at work or another busy activity.**

*(This decompression can take the form of napping, playing a video game, reading the paper or, as one women elegantly described her husband's downtime: staring at the bookcase for half an hour or so.)*

There are a whole lot of other differences, but these examples right here can easily turn into a relationship hornet's nest if neither side is seeking to understand where the other is coming from.

*"Hey honey, now that you're home from work, I need to talk about my feelings!"*

*"Not now, babe, I need to stare at the bookcase for a half hour or so."*

**Cue World War III.**

As if this weren't enough, the differences between men and women are compounded by our own individual differences AS WELL AS our differences in attachment styles.

## SECURE, ANXIOUS OR AVOIDANT

Again, from the book *Attached*, we learn that everyone falls into one of the three attachment styles: **Secure, Anxious** or **Avoidant** (or some combination of two), and these styles have an incredibly powerful effect on how we choose, relate to and exist in relationships.

Those with a secure bond find it relatively easy to trust and become close to a partner while those with an anxious attachment get very nervous when they don't receive constant attention or reinforcement.

On the other end of the spectrum, those with an avoidant attachment style have a hard time letting anyone get close to them and tend to sabotage relationships.

# The Five Love Languages

## GIVING AND RECEIVING LOVE

Convinced of the enormity of our differences yet? No? Here's more evidence.

Not only are we different as genders and different in our attachment styles, but we are also different in the way we best recognize and receive love. In our Power Players section on The Platinum Rule later in the book, we talk about *The Five Love Languages by Gary Chapman.*

We all have a favored way of receiving love, either in the form of:

### WORDS OF AFFIRMATION
*I love you now more than ever!*

### ACTS OF SERVICE
*Why don't you let me take the car today to get the oil changed?*

### RECEIVING GIFTS
*Look, I bought you a pretty new necklace!*

### QUALITY TIME
*Can we snuggle on the couch and watch a movie together tonight?*

### PHYSICAL TOUCH
*You've had a tough day, let me give you a foot rub.*

While all of those sound delightful to me (and I doubt anyone would balk at ANY of them), we definitely all have a preference for which we like best and if you are not picking up on your partner's love language, you're probably doing a lousy job of making them really happy.

**In short, you may be trying to make deposits, but they aren't resonating with your partner.**

**WORDS OF AFFIRMATION**

**ACTS OF SERVICE**

**RECEIVING GIFTS**

**QUALITY TIME**

**PHYSICAL TOUCH**

## BRINGING IT BACK TO ENGAGEMENT EQUITY

When you take all of these differences into account and then realize that you're relying on someone who probably see the world in a fundamentally different way for your major support system, you can see how things can go awry.

Which finally brings us to the whole point of this book. Engagement Equity is all about putting your ego and score-keeping aside and focusing on how you can improve the relationships and give value to the other person.

> "Happy couples are more concerned with being close than they are about being right."

**While a typical relationship can often look like this:**

*I came home from a busy day at work to the house being a complete pit even though I know John had the day off. I'm going to pout in my room, he can figure out dinner for himself.*

**A relationship focused on Engagement Equity turns into this:**

*I came home from a busy day at work to the house being a complete pit even though I know John had the day off. I know I have not been giving him a lot of love or attention lately because I've been focused on my career, so our account is probably overdrawn. I'm going to clean up and make him a nice dinner and make sure he knows I appreciate him supporting my work goals.*

Many of you busy women might want to slap me right now, and that's understandable. At first, it seems like giving in. And of course you're probably thinking that if you let the dirty house slide this time, he'll just keep doing it more and more because he can get away with it.

But it really comes down to this: in a healthy relationship, there is no score-keeping.

**Happy couples are more concerned with being close than they are about being right.**

## MAKING THE RIGHT DEPOSITS

Can this get lopsided if one person is focused on Engagement Equity and the other isn't?

Of course it can. This is not a magic pill that will instantly fix all of your relationship problems. But the beauty of living like this is that, more often than not, it causes the other person to change too.

Not because you're *telling* them to, simply because you've started treating them in a way that helps them be more secure, loving and open. *It just naturally happens.*

The deposits you make into a romantic relationship account are certainly going to look a little different than your other accounts (unless your co-worker really enjoys you offering to rub their feet after a difficult board meeting), but many of the same concepts apply.

- **Your partner wants to feel important.**

- **Your partner wants you to treat them as they would like to be treated.**

- **Your partner wants to feel you are interested in their life and their thoughts.**

- **Your partner wants you to share.**

- **Your partner wants you to really listen to them.**

However, romantic relationships are far more reliant on trust and on consistent, reliable actions that build that trust and closeness than any other relationship in our lives.

# How and When to Make Deposits in Your Romantic Relationships

## SLIDING DOOR MOMENTS

Brene Brown in her book *Daring Greatly* refers to an article by John Gottman, considered the country's foremost couples researcher. In his article, he tells about what he's learned about trust building:

> What I've found through research is that trust is built in very small moments, which I call 'sliding door' moments after the movie Sliding Doors. In any interaction, there is a possibility of connecting with your partner or turning away from your partner.
>
> Let me give you an example of that from my own relationship. One night, I really wanted to finish a mystery novel. I thought I knew who the killer was, but I was anxious to find out. At one point in the night, I put the novel on my bedside table and walked into the bathroom.
>
> As I passed the mirror, I saw my wife's face in reflection and she looked sad, brushing her hair. There was a sliding door moment.
>
> I had a choice. I could sneak out of the bathroom and think I don't want to deal with her sadness tonight; I want to read my novel. But instead, because I'm a sensitive researcher of relationships, I decided to go into the bathroom. I took the brush from her hand and asked, "What's the matter, baby?"
>
> And she told me why she was sad.
>
> Now, at that moment, I was building trust; I was there for her. I was connecting with her rather than choosing to think only about what I wanted. These are the moments, we've discovered, that build trust.
>
> One such moment is not that important, but if you're always choosing to turn away, then trust erodes in a relationship—very gradually, very slowly.

It really brings new meaning to the ancient term, '*death by a thousand cuts*'. By the time a relationship falls apart, you usually can't even identify what the big problem was.

It was just thousands upon thousands of these 'sliding door' moments where you or your partner chose to turn away.

## TURN AWAY NO LONGER

**When you're focused on Engagement Equity, you stop choosing to turn away.**

A deposit is synonymous with connecting, with walking into that bathroom instead of finishing your book. And the more deposits you make, the more trust you build.

# Engagement Equity in Relationships

**Write your responses to the questions below.**

## ROMANTIC RELATIONSHIPS EXERCISE

What is your partner's love language?

_____

_____

How are you making deposits in their account through the words or actions that mean the most to them?

_____

_____

_____

_____

What are some of your partner's favorite things? How often do you give him/her those things without first wondering what you will get in return? How could you give more?

_____

_____

_____

_____

Does your partner need downtime when he or she gets home from work? What can you do to create a space for them to decompress so you can come together later in the day for connection?

_____

_____

_____

_____

_____

_____

_____

_____

# Additional Notes

**Use this space for any additional takeaways learned from this activity.**

# CHAPTER FIVE

# Engagement Equity in Friendships

## BUILDING EQUITY IN FRIENDSHIPS

Having friends is incredibly important, which is something I've always known. However, until I started doing some research for this chapter of the book, I don't think I was quite aware of exactly HOW incredibly important they really are.

Yes, we think of friends as an extended support system, people to go out and have fun with and maybe someone we can cry to when our relationship isn't going so hot or our kids ask us to drop them off two blocks from school.

According to Carlin Flora, author of *Friendfluence: The Surprising Ways Friends Make Us Who We Are*, friendships have evolved from having a mostly protective effect (when our ancestors lived in clans or small villages, friends helped to protect us from the enemy as well as hunt and gather food) to being critical for much of our emotional and social development.

**Friends can be our main source of moral support, the champion of our dreams and our confidantes.** They also have a huge influence on our happiness and can even increase our intelligence.

> "
> Friendship is born at the moment when one person says to another 'What! You too? I thought that no one but myself...'
>
> **C.S. LEWIS**

## FRIENDSHIPS ARE DIFFERENT

I could go on and on about how important friendships are to our lives, but that's not what this book is about. If you're reading this, you already *know* how important friendships are and you're more interested in finding out how to be a better friend (or how to find friends who are better for *you*).

Friendships are tricky and are wholly different from the other relationships (co-workers, employees, spouses, children, business prospects) we talk about in this book.

Why are they so different? It boils down to one simple reason: **friendships are almost entirely built on choice.**

You cannot choose your parents or which children you bear. Many times, you cannot choose who your boss is or the co-workers you must interact with daily. And, after that initial choice when you say 'I do', you can no longer choose your spouse (well, you CAN, but for the purpose of this chapter lets assume you marry only once in your life and stay together 'til death do you part.)

## FRIENDSHIP IS A CHOICE

Because they are based on choice, many people find themselves constantly questioning the friends they have, if they should remain friends with them, how to make more friends, and which friends to hang out with on a Saturday night.

While you will (hopefully) never hear, "Honey, I just don't think Johnny is measuring up. Should we drop him and think about getting a new son?" You may very well have heard (or said) something similar about a friend many, many times.

And because there is so much choice involved when it comes to friendship, it can become incredibly easy to adopt a 'tit for tat' mindset when it comes to them and unnecessarily drop friends for 'not reciprocating' instead of focusing on how you personally can add value to the relationship.

**Consider this excerpt, again from *Friendfluence*:**

> For decades, evolutionary biologists believed friendship to be a function of reciprocal exchange: as long as the back-scratching escalates at a mutually beneficial rate, the friends get chummier.
>
> In the late '90s, psychologists John Tooby, Ph.D., and Leda Cosmides, Ph.D., began exploring other reasons we've evolved to be altruistic—why we help others even at our own expense.
>
> Tooby and Cosmides noticed that most people got angry when they heard the standard explanation that friendship is a tit-for-tat enterprise.
>
> They denied their own friendships were based solely on favor trading, and they insisted that they greatly enjoyed lending a hand to those they care about.
>
> 'Indeed,' the researchers write in one of their papers, 'explicit linkage between favors or insistence by a recipient that she be allowed to immediately 'repay' are generally taken as signs of a lack of friendship'.

## TIT FOR TAT ISN'T A FRIENDSHIP

That's right. When asked, people thought that insisting on reciprocation in a relationship was not the basis of it, but instead indicated that there *was* no friendship. Which really makes complete sense when you think about it.

## "I did this for you, when are you going to do something for me?"

If you immediately feel the need to take Sally to lunch because she's brought you a breakfast muffin and coffee, you're doing so because you don't feel like you will have a chance to repay Sally later on in your friendship.

Instead, you want to repay her *immediately* (before she can tell everyone she knows that she brought you breakfast and you never did anything for her in return).

However, if you and Sally are chums, you'll remember that you bought Sally a drink at last month's wedding reception and that you have plans for a movie night coming up and that you'll be the one providing the snacks.

While this makes a whole lot of sense when you think about it, we still tend to drift back to that '*I did this for you, when are you going to do something for me?*' mentality.

Consider the popular site The Friendship Blog, created by "The Friendship Doctor" and author of *Best Friends Forever,* Irene S. Levine, Ph.D. What do you think is one of the biggest friendship complaints she sees in her forum?

People felt like they were putting more work into a friendship than the other person. Yep, it pretty much came down to keeping score.

Now, while we'll never advocate letting yourself be a doormat or continuing to work on an essentially dead relationship (see chapter on 'Closing the Account'), **you'll have to admit that always focusing on an even relationship is NOT the path to happiness.**

# Why is focusing on 'tit for tat' such a bad idea in friendships? Consider this...

## WE ALL HAVE OUR OWN LIVES AND OTHER PRIORITIES OFTEN COME FIRST

While you may be vividly aware that you've invited Jenny to lunch twice, the movies once and out for drinks while she's not invited you to do anything. Jenny may be so preoccupied with her kids, her career and her needy husband that she has no clue there's some invitation inequality going on.

## WE TEND TO PERSONALIZE THINGS

While you might still be holding a grudge about how you bought Gretchen a $50 massage for her birthday and she only gave you a card for yours, the truth of the matter could be that Gretchen is experiencing money troubles and was too embarrassed to tell you. Many of us take imagined slights to heart when in fact none are intended.

Another reason that many of us don't even realize comes from Marla Paul, author of *The Friendship Crisis*.

She explains:

> People have wildly varying social appetites. Some are voracious eaters, heaping their plates with huge portions from a giant buffet of pals. Others are nibblers, easily sated with a bite here and there. Understanding those differences may illuminate—and depersonalize—why some women rarely pick up the phone or embrace an overture of friendship.

You might be thinking Cassie is a bad friend because you're always calling her and she rarely calls you, when in actuality, that's just Cassie's friendship personality. She likes you just fine, she just doesn't need the same amount of 'friend stimuli' as you do.

# Instead of Constantly Worrying About the Day-to-Day Score Keeping, You Can Focus on Making Deposits

## ENGAGEMENT EQUITY WITH FRIENDS

So what does this all boil down to? Well, it all comes back to building our equity accounts with our friends.

Depending on how large your circle of close friends is (depending on your 'friendship personality' and your level of extro- or introversion, this could be as small as one or two or as large as 20+), you need to establish an equity account with each one of them and then you need to start making deposits.

**Imagine the relief of being able to stop wondering:**

*"I already invited Cindy to drinks twice and she's never invited me to do anything. Is it really worth it to invite her again?"*

If you've already established your good friendships (or have determined some new 'friend potentials' that you know are worth investing in), you can stop worrying about the day-to-day score keeping because, let's face it, that gets *exhausting*.

**No longer constantly wonder:**

*"Is he going to repay that favor?"*

*"What did she mean by that text?"*

*"She forgot my birthday, does she not care about me?"*

*"Did they not accept my invitation because they have something better to do with other friends?"*

## FRIENDSHIP DEPOSITS

What does a deposit into a friendship account look like? And are all deposits equal?

Again, the focus here should not be on score-keeping and instead should focus on the individual and the value you can bring to his or her life.

**Do you have a friend who is a busy working mom who rarely takes time for herself?**

Deposits into her account might take the form of offering to watch the kids so she can have a night out with her husband, giving her a book related to her career you know would interest her and an invitation for a happy hour glass of wine to unwind from a long day.

**Maybe you have an old college buddy you remain close to.**

Deposits into his account could be a round of golf on a Sunday afternoon, an invite to watch the big game at your house and a bottle of his favorite scotch on his birthday.

## RELATIONSHIPS ARE UNIQUE

Friendships are dynamic, unique relationships and no two are alike.

An equity account between you and one of your friends may look wildly different from another *and that's okay.*

The important thing is to make your deposits based on that relationship and the special energy, history and shared interests the two of you have developed.

If you've been burned by a friend (and really, almost all of us have), you might be a little concerned at this point.

If you are completely focused on giving, won't you be taken advantage of?

There is always that chance, yes. Especially if you've got some friendships that probably needed pruning anyway. However, what you'll most likely find is that giving begets more giving.

The more you make deposits into their accounts, the more they'll deposit in return. They may not even realize they're doing it, it's simply a reaction.

And the result?

**Stronger, less exhausting friendships that achieve all of the goals we had when we became friends in the first place.**

"

You can make more friends in two months by becoming interested in other people than you can in two years by trying to get other people interested in you.

**DALE CARNEGIE**

# CHAPTER SIX

# Engagement Equity in Parenting

## BUILDING EQUITY IN PARENTING

Is there any area of life where there is more conflicting advice than parenting? Let babies cry, soothe them as soon as they are upset, put ironclad rules in place, be more open and flexible, be their best friend, no don't be their best friend be their parent... etc. etc. etc.

If you start getting into all the research and advice and how-to books, it's very easy to get overwhelmed, exhausted and left with one thought:

*"Wow, I'm a crappy parent."*

The whole parenting advice realm has gotten out of control.

**Parenting a child in one correct way is simply not possible.** We all have different ways of parenting, different styles and quirks based on our community, our religion, our own upbringing and a hundred other factors. Are they different? Yes. Does that make any of them right or any of them *wrong*? No.

Well, we obviously know that there are PLENTY of *wrong* ways to parent, but for this chapter we are focused on those who are interested in trying their best to be good parents.

> **"**
>
> How do we communicate worthiness to our children? Only through our presence: our full-on, engaged, attuned presences.
>
> **DR. SHEFALI TSABARY**

# Disapproval, Annoyance and Criticism, No Matter What Positive Motivation is Behind Them, Are Withdrawals

## PARENTING IS A TWO-WAY STREET

Many times, we forget that our relationship with our children is a dynamic two-way street. Yes, we are the parent but that does not mean that our relationship involves just telling our kids what to do and showing them how to become an adult.

We have an equity account with each of our children, and to get the most out of that relationship, we need to be making as many deposits into it as any other account we have.

Fortunately, making deposits into your child's account isn't really that difficult. In fact, the simplest things often make the biggest impacts.

Consider this quote from Toni Morrison that Brene Brown wrote about in her book *Daring Greatly*:

> Ms. Morrison explained that it's interesting to watch what happens when a child walks into a room. She asked, 'Does your face light up?'

> She explained, 'When my children used to walk in the room when they were little, I looked at them to see if they had buckled their trousers or if their hair was combed or if their socks were up... You think your affection and deep love is on display because you're caring for them. It's not. When they see you, they see the critical face. What's wrong now?

Let your face speak what's in your heart. When they walk in the room my face says I'm glad to see them. It's just as small as that, you see?'

**Wow. Isn't that powerful?**

While we're focused on making sure they don't look like they were raised by wolves, all they see is the criticism on our faces. Your caring for them turns from a deposit (as you intended) into a withdrawal.

## MAKING A DEPOSIT IN YOUR CHILD'S ACCOUNT

**I have my own example of this that shows how innate this behavior is.**

My daughter spends one evening during the week with her father and he brings her to school the next morning.

He's a great dad and loves our daughter very much, but like many fathers, he struggles with things like outfits, hair combing and deodorants.

On this particular day, my daughter was in the small lunchroom where her after school program meets. It was one of the first days of the school year, so many of the staff at the after school program were new and did not know me or my daughter well yet.

Listen earnestly to anything your children want to tell you, no matter what. If you don't listen eagerly to the little stuff when they are little, they won't tell you the big stuff when they are big, because to them all of it has always been big stuff.

**CATHERINE M. WALLACE**

I walked in, excited to hear how my daughter's day was, when I saw her trotting toward me in pink floral pants that were two sizes too small and an oversized blue and green striped boys t-shirt.

Before I could even think, I blurted (with a horrified look on my face): *'Well that's an interesting outfit!'*

Immediately, I recognized my folly and clapped a hand over my mouth, but the damage was done.

While this was going through my head: *"Oh my gosh, did the other kids make fun of her? Was she embarrassed in front of her new teacher?"*, this was probably going through hers: *"Why isn't Mom happy to see me?"*

## PARENTING WITHDRAWALS

Disapproval, annoyance and criticism, no matter what positive motivation is behind them, are withdrawals.

On the other hand, joy, happiness and encouragement are deposits.

**That's right: just expressing happiness at being with your child is, in and of itself, a huge deposit into their account.**

# How to Leave Meaningful, Worthwhile Deposits in Your Child's Account

## EXAMPLES OF PARENTING DEPOSITS

What are some of the other big-time players in parental Engagement Equity? Brene Brown explains:

> Engagement means investing time and energy. It means sitting down with our children and understanding their worlds, their interests, and their stories. Engaged parents can be found on both sides of all of the controversial parenting debates. They come from different values, traditions and cultures.

> What they share in common is practicing the values. What they seem to share is the philosophy of "I'm not perfect and I'm not always right, but I'm here, open, paying attention, loving you and fully engaged."

**Just showing your kids that you know you'll make mistakes but that you're also going to continue to show up and TRY is huge.**

She also references C.R. Snyder's research on hope and quotes:

> To learn hopefulness, children need relationships that are characterized by boundaries, consistency and support.

When we set boundaries for our kids (no matter how much they may protest or pout), we are making a deposit.

When they know that action A always leads to consequence B, we are making a deposit.

And when we support them in their efforts (even if those efforts aren't something that we necessarily would like them to focus on), we make a deposit. It sounds so easy, doesn't it?

But we all know it *isn't.*

If it were that easy, we'd all be super parents raising incredibly well-adjusted, happy, productive members of society. I think we can all agree that's not happening.

## ENGAGEMENT EQUITY IN PARENTING

Will focusing on Engagement Equity with your child ensure that he or she will not struggle or rebel or have major issues in life? Of course not.

But focusing on making deposits can have a big impact on your child's sense of security, which affects the way they interact with people and situations and the world in general.

## THEY ARE NOT THEIR MISTAKES

When we focus more on what we are giving our children (and I'm not talking about gifts) and less on how to make them behave, achieve or fit in, we're showing them we care more about *them* than *what they do*.

**This sounds baffling at first. Aren't those the same thing? But they're not (or shouldn't be).**

If your child drops a glass and breaks it, he made a clumsy mistake. If you react to the incident by calling *him* clumsy, you are not only making a withdrawal, you are also making him believe that HE is synonymous with HIS MISTAKES.

- **I say dumb things sometimes. I am NOT dumb.**

- **I get busy and neglect calling my friends back sometimes. I am NOT a neglectful friend.**

- **I can become insecure and need reassurances in some situations. I am NOT needy.**

Do you see the difference? We need to help our kids see the difference as well.

## PAVING THE WAY

Another huge issue gluing Engagement Equity and parenting together can be summed up in one word: *modeling*.

Do we want our kids to interact with the world with kindness and understanding and with a focus on giving value to those in their lives?

Of course we do.

What is the one biggest determining factor

> "Many times, not *walking the walk* comes down to neglecting the Radiate Outward principle."

whether they will do that or not?

**It's how they see us interacting with the world.**

We can tell our kids how to act and how to treat other people over and over, but what if they see us walking a different walk?

Not only are you showing them inconsistency, but you're also negating all of the lessons you're trying to teach them.

For example, if you are constantly telling your kids to treat everyone equally, yet you make negative comments about those of other races or backgrounds, you are being inconsistent and confusing.

Many times, not *walking the walk* comes down to neglecting the Radiate Outward principle (described on page 64).

If you tell your kids they are the most important things in the world to you, yet miss dinner four nights a week because you're working late, you're making withdrawals from their account.

# Engagement Equity in Parenting

## PARENTING EXERCISE

Make time to sit down with each of your children for 20 minutes this week. Engage them in conversation and learn more about what they like, who their friends are, their goals and dreams.

Don't judge anything they say, simply listen and ask questions to learn more.

Use the lines on this page to take notes about how each session went.

_____
_____
_____
_____
_____
_____
_____
_____
_____
_____
_____
_____
_____
_____
_____
_____
_____
_____
_____
_____
_____
_____
_____
_____
_____

# CHAPTER SEVEN

# Engagement Equity with Strangers

## ENGAGEMENT EQUITY WITH STRANGERS

Okay, okay, the title of this chapter might sound weird. You are probably thinking, *"Why in the world would I need to establish an equity account with someone I've never seen before and may never see again?"*

Before you skip this chapter altogether, let's think for a moment about everyone special in your life to whom you are NOT biologically related. What do every single one of these people have in common?

**At one time, they were strangers.**

Yes, even your beloved spouse and best friend, at one time, was that completely unfamiliar weirdo who walked into your 6th grade homeroom or asked to be your partner in yoga class.

And consider what your life would look like now if you'd completely ostracized THEM and not let them become a part of your life! Yep, I think you can now agree that developing some type of engagement strategy with strangers can be a very good idea.

However, it's about much more than just investing in an unknown account and hoping it will grow into something more. But before we go there, let's take a look at why we're so averse to connecting with strangers in the first place.

## GETTING TO KNOW A STRANGER

Let's go back to the days when we were primitive humans living in small groups or villages. If someone waltzed up to us who was NOT part of our small group, it was pretty likely that that person was not there to introduce himself and suggest you go out to Starbucks to get to know each other better.

Nope, in those times, it was extremely likely that that person was there to *kill* you and take all your animal skins.

Or your pottery.

Or whatever it was you were into.

We developed a fear of strangers and those who are different from us *for a reason.*

Even in this day and age, where we're no longer worried that every new person we see is going to steal our animal skins, we're wired from an early age to trust those we know and avoid those we don't.

## ATTACHMENT THEORY

In the chapter on Engagement Equity in relationships, we talked about attachment theory.

*Attachment theory* states that we learn how to grow and interact with the world by forming a strong, secure base with a parent (or parent figure) when we are infants.

If we form this secure base, we're better able to go out in the world and take chances and learn new things because we know we can always come back to our secure base if things get tough out there.

However, as adults, this attachment can sometimes work against us because we are programmed to seek solace and comfort in those we know and have already formed a strong bond with.

> "We're wired from an early age to trust those we know and avoid those we don't."

Though this does help us to go out and try to conquer the world in business or have the courage to sky dive, it may hamper us in trying to form bonds with those we are unfamiliar with.

So as you can see, this is all well and good when you're an infant.

Or a caveman.

But it starts NOT serving us so well in the modern age of adulthood when we could gain a good many things from strangers if we just weren't so uncomfortable around them.

## STRANGERS BECOME MORE

**As we stated before, almost all of the important people in our lives started out as strangers.**

And except for those few lightning bolt moments when we recall someone walking in a room and knowing we would have this person in our lives forever, we mostly don't know who those people are going to be.

> "When we limit our engagement to those we already know well, we severely impact our ability to expand our circles."

The rude chick who seems to be judging your outfit could just be having a bad day and will end up being one of your closest friends.

The surly and suspicious prospect could become your very best client and the guy in the goofy hat with the snorting laugh could very well become your husband.

When we are limiting our engagement to those we already know well, we are severely impacting our ability to expand our circles.

When we don't give others a chance to be our new friends or possible business partners or mates, it's like closing up the doors and barring all the windows.

## STRANGERS HELP US GROW

In his book *The Necessity of Strangers*, Alan Gregerman makes some fascinating points about how strangers help us grow and succeed:

Your friends and existing networks are tremendous assets in your growth and success, but they're simply not enough.

Sometimes they are too much like you to help in solving pressing problems or creating new opportunities, and sometimes they are just too likely to confirm the things you already think or believe.

And besides, relying only on friends and colleagues limits your access to a world of cool and powerful ideas—even if you are among the best connected people on the planet

Imagine that you could connect with anyone in the world, wouldn't that be awesome?

Well today you can, and you can combine what others know with the best of what your friends, coworkers, neighbors, and other contacts know to realize your full potential.

And all it takes is a sense of curiosity and openness.

We tend to hang out with those we like (hopefully), and what do the people we like mostly have in common?

**Research has shown that we gravitate toward those who are similar to us, who share the same beliefs, experiences and mindsets.**

This makes for some pleasant dinner conversation and might save us from arguing over which movie to see, but it hinders us when we need to see something from a different perspective.

It also isn't so helpful in pushing us outside our comfort zone to seek new experiences or think about an issue in a way we would never have considered.

## STRANGERS SHOW US NEW EXPERIENCES

There's fascinating evidence about why Steve Jobs was one of the *most innovative* thinkers in recent history.

The main reason why he was able to come up with the ideas he did was due to his **multitude of various experiences in his lifetime.**

He learned about new subjects, tried new hobbies and sought out people who were as different from him as possible.

Steve was able to think the way he did because he was *constantly exposing himself to strangers* (in a good way, not the type of way that would have led to jail time).

## CONNECTING WITH STRANGERS HELPS MAKE OUR LIVES EASIER

**(And everyone's life happier!)**

Have you ever been treated rudely by a store clerk or a customer service rep on the phone?

Have you wondered why the kid handing your hamburger through the drive-through window is giving you the stink-eye?

> "We're treated rudely by strangers... because they are used to being treated rudely by those they serve."

More often than not, we're treated rudely by strangers in the customer service industry because they are used to being treated rudely by those they serve.

*Why is that customer service rep yelling at you?*

It could very well be because he was yelled at all morning by other customers for situations that weren't his fault.

The store clerk is so used to customers yapping away on their cell phones while they check out that she no longer even tries to be nice.

And yep, the kid at the drive-through window believes that approximately 0% of those he serves are going to make eye contact or thank him, so he simply prepares himself for the brush-off before he even opens his window.

Consider this personal story from Brene Brown:

> After leaving Barnes & Noble, I went to a drive-through fast food restaurant to get a Diet Dr. Pepper.
>
> Right as I pulled up to the window, my cell phone rang. I wasn't quite sure, but I thought it might be my son's school calling, so I answered it.
>
> It wasn't the school—it was someone calling to confirm an appointment. I got off the phone as quickly as I could.
>
> In the short time it took me to say, "Yes, I'll be at my appointment," the woman in the window and I had finished our soda-for-money transaction.
>
> I apologized to her the second I got off of that phone. I said, "I'm so sorry. The phone rang right when I was pulling up and I thought it was my son's school."
>
> I must have surprised her because she got huge tears in her eyes and said, "Thank you. Thank you so much. You have no idea how humiliating it is sometimes. They don't even see us."

## ENGAGEMENT EQUITY WITH STRANGERS

Now, I'm not saying that your reaching out and attempting a little Engagement Equity with people in the customer service industry is going to negate all the other people who treat them like they don't exist. But it just might make the next person's experience a little better.

And if more and more of us do it, then the next time you need to call up the utility company with a question about your bill, that rep is going to try a little harder to help you out because they haven't been consistently treated like garbage.

And even if it doesn't? Well, treating people who you'll probably never see or talk to again with respect is just the decent thing to do. We forget that sometimes.

**So what does Engagement Equity with strangers look like?**

It's clearly got to be different, right?

After all, we're talking about people we don't know and who we may never see again.

However, many of the same *Power Players* that we'll talk about in the next section work with those we're close to as well as strangers. Sometimes they just need a little tweaking.

66

Smile at strangers and you just might change a life.

**STEVE MARABOLI**

## LISTENING

Just making sure you limit distractions and look a cashier in the eye when they're asking you if you want paper or plastic is a deposit.

## CURIOSITY

Ask someone you've just met at a conference where they found that beautiful scarf they're wearing and really listen to the answer. If they say, *"Target,"* ask a follow-up question, *"Is that one of your favorite colors? It looks great on you!"*

## PRACTICE THE GOLDEN RULE

Because we don't know how strangers want to be treated, we can fall back on the good ol' Golden Rule. Would you want someone to yell at you on the phone if you were trying to make their Wi-Fi work? Didn't think so.

## THE ASK (OR TAKING WITHDRAWALS)

This is another tricky one because you often don't have the chance to get to an ask with strangers because your interactions with them are limited. But in one-time interactions, you can still operate on the 3-4 deposits for one withdrawal. **For example:**

> **Cashier:** *Would you like paper or plastic?*
>
> **You:** *(Looking them in the eyes)* DEPOSIT
>
> I'll take paper, Melody, thank you! DEPOSIT  I love your bracelet, by the way. Where did you get it? DEPOSIT
>
> **Cashier:** Oh, thank you! My mother gave it to me.
>
> **You:** Well, it's beautiful. Hey, would you mind double-bagging the ice cream? I have a few stops to make before I get home. WITHDRAWAL

Most of the time, Engagement Equity with strangers comes down to two simple things: *Curiosity* and common courtesy.

Employ these with anyone you meet and you'll likely be well ahead of most people they meet on a daily basis.

**LISTENING**

**CURIOSITY**

**PLATINUM RULE**

**THE ASK**

# CHAPTER EIGHT

# The Key to Engagement Equity: Radiate Outwards

## RADIATING OUTWARDS

Have you ever known someone who is a pillar of the community, always willing to lend a hand to a stranger, is at every important event to support colleagues... and yet has a bitter wife, rebellious children and resentful employees?

Believe me, I've known a lot of people like this. From an outside perspective, they seem to be the epitome of Engagement Equity, but when you dig a little deeper, you see they aren't using it where it matters most.

The goal of Engagement Equity is not to gain the admiration of everyone around you or to get your name in the paper—though that may happen if you do it correctly.

The goal is to have a happy, fulfilled life where you are giving and receiving encouragement, love and support. For that to really work, you have to start closest to home in both your business and professional life and then let your actions radiate outward.

So yes, you need to focus on your family and your business, but that's the *second* layer of Engagement Equity.

The center of the entire concept is about one person: you.

> "
> To be a strong person for others, we must first be a strong person for ourselves.
>
> **BRENE BROWN**

# You Are The Center of Engagement Equity!

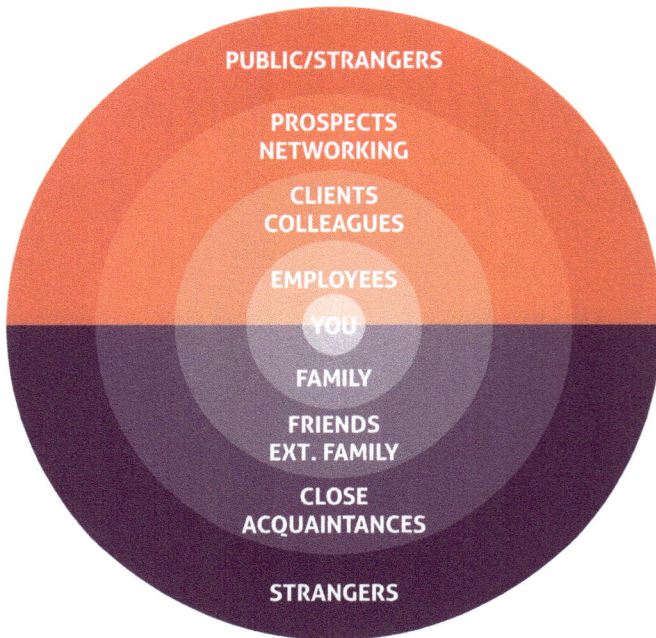

Concentric circles diagram with YOU at the center. Radiating outward in the orange (upper) half: EMPLOYEES, CLIENTS COLLEAGUES, PROSPECTS NETWORKING, PUBLIC/STRANGERS. Radiating outward in the purple (lower) half: FAMILY, FRIENDS EXT. FAMILY, CLOSE ACQUAINTANCES, STRANGERS.

## RADIATING OUTWARDS

We've all been on a plane and heard the safety briefing on securing our own oxygen masks before helping others with theirs, right?

If you've read a lot of self-help books or been to seminars, you've probably heard this as an analogy for self-care and it rings true in every facet of life.

You simply cannot help others if you are doing it from a place of weakness, emptiness or lack of self love.

If you don't take care of yourself first, you'll fall into the dreaded martyr or co-dependent roles that will ultimately drain you and push others away.

**To be a strong person for others, we must first be a strong person for ourselves.**

Consider this quote from Brene Brown in her wonderful book *Braving the Wilderness: The Quest for True Belonging and the Courage to Stand Alone*:

> True belonging is the spiritual practice of believing in and belonging to yourself so deeply that you can share your most authentic self with the world and find sacredness in both being a part of something and standing alone in the wilderness.
>
> True belonging doesn't require you to change who you are; it requires you to be who you are.

## PERSONAL ENGAGEMENT EQUITY

Just as we have with others, we have an Engagement Equity bank with ourselves.

We put in deposits when we get enough sleep, exercise, take 'me' time, and engage in hobbies and activities that bring us joy.

We withdraw from our account when we say yes when we really want to say no, when we take on too much or when we put off something that is meaningful or important to us to help others.

**These withdrawals are going to be necessary, of course, but they'll start to drain us if we aren't also making the appropriate number of deposits.**

## RELATIONSHIPS: THE SECOND LAYER

Once we've ensured our account with ourselves is in the black, we can move on to the next layer. In our personal lives, that consists of our families.

> "Radiating outward is a way to put first things first and keep your priorities in line."

Are we making frequent deposits into our kids' and significant other's account? Are they getting enough time, love and attention from us? Yes? Great, then we can move on to friends. You see where I'm going here?

It's the same with your business. You come first because a leader cannot be at his or her best if they aren't taking care of themselves. Their employees come next.

Too many leaders skip this step altogether and spend most of their time pleasing clients or running after that next sale or speaking engagement while their neglected employees wonder if they should be looking for a new job.

You have to make sure your employees' accounts are in good shape before you move on or your business will crumble from the inside out.

## ACQUAINTANCES AND STRANGERS: THE FINAL LAYER

It's only after you've covered yourself, your loved ones and those you have strong relationships with that you can move onto acquaintances, prospects and strangers. When you approach them with a solid positive balance in all your other accounts, you can do so out of a giving spirit instead of trying to gain something from them to fill a hole in your life.

You'll also know that any time you spend making deposits into their accounts is not time you're taking away from someone else who needs it more.

**Radiating outward is a way to put first things first and keep your priorities in line.**

When you start getting positive feedback from putting the Engagement Equity concept in place, it can be easy to lose sight of what's really important and start going for the low-hanging fruit of those who will give you the most compliments or gratitude.

Though it might feel good at the time, it's not going to lead to long-term fulfillment as those relationships most important to you will suffer.

# CHAPTER NINE

# Engagement Equity Power Players

## ENGAGEMENT EQUITY POWER PLAYERS

So you get the whole Engagement Equity concept, right?

You see how it plays out in your personal and business life and you understand how making deposits into accounts 80% of the time and making withdrawals 20% of the time makes sense.

However, it can be tough to know sometimes what makes a good deposit into someone's account. So now let's go into some specific 'deposits' you can work on.

I call these "**Power Players**" because they tend to make a big impact on those you use them with—especially if you do so on a consistent basis.

> "
>
> Great power involves great responsibility.
>
> **FRANKLIN D. ROOSEVELT**

# Listening is One of The Absolute Best Deposits You Can Make Into Anyone's Account

**LISTENING**

## POWER PLAYER 1: LISTENING

As we continue to talk about Engagement Equity and the power of making deposits into business and personal accounts, one of the pitfalls that often occurs is that **we start thinking too much.**

We make detailed lists of how we can make deposits, come up with gifts we can give or referrals we can make or articles we can share that will account for the multitude of deposits we need to continually make.

It doesn't have to be that difficult, people!

You know one of the absolute best deposits you can make into anyone's account, whether it's a child, a business prospect, a friend or a co-worker?

**It's just one word: listen.**

Now, before you start becoming defensive and insist that you are always listening, that you feel you spend big chunks of your day listening to others, consider the following:

*A study of over 8,000 people employed in business, hospitals, universities, the military and government agencies found that virtually all of the respondents believed that they communicate as effectively or more effectively than their co-workers.*

**(Could everyone be above average?)**

*However, research shows that the average person listens at only about 25% efficiency. While most people agree that listening effectively is a very important skill, most people don't feel a strong need to improve their own skill level.*

# Where Listening Goes Wrong

**Hmmm, we're only listening with 25% efficiency? What in the world are we doing the other 75% percent of the time?**

Research (and personal observation) shows that it's some combination of the following:

## 1. SPACING OFF

## 2. ARGUING WITH THE OTHER PERSON IN YOUR HEAD

## 3. THINKING ABOUT SOMETHING COMPLETELY DIFFERENT

*For some reason I tend to think about what I'm going to cook for dinner that night when I find myself disconnecting from a conversation.*

## 4. DOING SOMETHING COMPLETELY DIFFERENT

*Have you ever nodded and said 'mmm hmmm' while you were working on your computer or watching TV? I know I have.*

## 5. PLANNING WHAT YOU'RE GOING TO SAY WHEN THE OTHER PERSON FINALLY SHUTS THEIR TRAP

*This is a big one!*

Most of us may start to listen to what the other person is saying, but then our minds immediately jump to a personal story, experience, etc. that we can talk about as soon as this other person is finished.

It's a natural reaction, since humankind is a self-centered breed. I don't mean that in an awful way, it's just the way we are.

Everyone, at the core, is more concerned with themselves than with anyone else. We can train ourselves to be better, of course, but that is just a natural tendency.

# How to Listen to Others

## SO HOW DO YOU REALLY LISTEN TO SOMEONE?

If you're doing one of the first four things in our list, the answer is pretty simple: **stop doing it and focus.**

It doesn't matter that you'd rather debate the merits of sweet potatoes vs. turnips to go with your burgers than hear about your co-worker's problems with her puppy. **TUNE IN and start making those deposits.**

If you find yourself facing the last issue, *waiting for your turn to talk,* which many of us are numerous times on a daily basis, take a pointer from Daniel Pink's book *To Sell is Human.*

Daniel wants to know how to be a better listener (and salesperson) and so he attends a seminar where they go through a number of different exercises.

He's paired with a stranger and they are instructed to each share something personal with their partner. Their partner is then required to offer a thoughtful response... but not until they wait for 20 seconds.

That might sound silly, but think about it! If you know that you're going to:

- **Have to respond to what they said instead of saying something about yourself and**

- **Wait 20 seconds before you can do it**

You've immediately removed any reason to be thinking about what you can say about yourself while the other person is talking!

While you may not be able to replicate this 100% in the real world, you can at least modify it a bit.

## NORMAL SCENARIO:

Jane at the office is telling you about the puppy she just got the week before. It's piddling on the rug, waking her up in the middle of the night and generally making her wonder if this was such a good idea.

While you do not have a puppy now, you remember the one that you had while in your first apartment and what a pain it was in the beginning, but how with a little patience and training, ol'Rover ended up being your best friend and companion for 12 years.

You begin figuring out a way to tell Jane about your experience so she'll see that, though it may be rough now, it's definitely worth it. Unfortunately, you haven't heard a word JANE has said since, "Maybe I should have gotten a cat instead!"

## REVISITED SCENARIO:

Jane starts talking about her puppy and, while your mind still immediately jumps to your experience with Rover, you know that you need to offer some thoughtful feedback on Jane's concerns and that you need to pause before you do so.

This makes you put the story of Rover in the back of your mind for the time being, and you actually pay attention to all of Jane's concerns.

You realize that her real issue is not that she doesn't think the puppy is worth it, it's that she just needed some reassurance.

Now you can pause and come up with some thoughtful feedback addressing Jane's real problem, instead of just blurting out your personal story that probably would have only made her feel worse.

## USING POWER PLAYER 1

**Listening—*really listening*—is an incredible powerful tool that can be used with absolutely anyone in your life.**

> "There can be no understanding without listening."

One of our greatest desires as human beings is to be understood, and **there can be no understanding without listening.**

And, as is the case with all Engagement Equity, the more you find yourself practicing good listening (DEPOSIT), the more you can expect to be rewarded when you ask someone to listen to you (WITHDRAWAL).

**SHARING**

## POWER PLAYER 2: SHARING

One of the most interesting things that has come out of our research on Engagement Equity is the realization that what we often think of as withdrawals are actually deposits and vice versa.

As we saw in the chapter on social media, many restaurants think they are giving value or making a deposit when they share a happy hour special, but they are actually 'asking' their followers to come in and spend money with them, so it's considered a withdrawal.

**Sharing is on the opposite end of the spectrum.**

When we talk about sharing, we're not referring to sharing your lunch with your co-worker or sharing your lawn tools with your neighbor *(though you would probably be a good guy to sit or live next to if you did).*

Instead, we're talking about **sharing something of yourself.**

When we share fears or memories or painful past experiences, we are letting people in.

And if you haven't noticed by this point in your life, there are many, many people who are terrified of letting others in.

In fact, it's quite likely you might be one of them. I know it's something I've needed to work on!

# Where Sharing Goes Wrong

**Why is sharing so difficult?**

A lot of it has to do with how introverted or extroverted we are: some people are just more open than others. However, that's only part of the story.

Here are some other common reasons why opening up and sharing with others is such an obstacle:

## WE DON'T WANT TO BURDEN OTHERS WITH OUR FEELINGS OR STORIES

This is a common reaction from introverts or those who feel they always need to take care of others.

We don't feel that others would be interested in hearing what we have to say, or feel that they have enough on their plate without having to share our worries or fears.

## WE DON'T WANT TO FEEL JUDGED

More than likely, at some point in your past, you've shared something painful or deeply personal with someone and they judged you for it.

Depending on how emotionally resilient you are (and who the judger was), you could have brushed this off or you could have let it affect you to the point where you're afraid to share and be judged again.

## WE DON'T WANT TO CHANGE

If you share with someone that you hate your job or that your spouse is making you miserable or that you feel awful about your weight, they may try to help you change. And deep down, perhaps you aren't ready to make those changes yet.

Not telling others how unhappy you are with an aspect of your life means you've got no accountability if you continue down the same path.

## WE WANT EVERYONE TO THINK WE'RE PERFECT

When you don't share past failures, embarrassments, mistakes or tough emotions with others, it's often because you don't want them to see you as flawed.

This happens a lot with parents or leaders. They think they need to look strong and infallible to their children or employees to give them a sense of security but instead it makes others feel like they cannot make mistakes or be less than perfect themselves.

## WE DON'T KNOW THE APPROPRIATE PEOPLE TO SHARE WITH

Sometimes, it's pretty easy to identify those in your life you should be sharing intimate thoughts with: a mate or a best friend you've had since childhood are natural choices.

However, once you get outside that very tight inner circle, the 'rules' get a little murkier.

Which friends should you tell about your abusive first marriage? Should you share only work stories with your co-workers or colleagues or can you talk about personal information?

This is a common issue because none of us want to be that 'oversharer' who we've all met.

## SHARE WITH THOSE WHO HAVE EARNED THE RIGHT TO HEAR IT

The key to effective sharing is to do so with those who earned the right to hear your stories. These are the people who have proven they are more than passing acquaintances, who've earned your trust and who have shared some of themselves with you.

When you share with these people, you deepen the relationships. When you don't share with those who have earned the right, you keep the relationships on a surface level.

Eventually, those people will stop sharing with you as well and the relationships will end.

## FLOODLIGHTING

Brene Brown refers to oversharing as *'floodlighting'* in her book *Daring Greatly*:

'Floodlighting' is where we use vulnerability as a manipulation tool. When we use vulnerability to floodlight our listener, the response is disconnection.

To understand floodlighting, we have to see that the intentions behind this kind of sharing are multifaceted and often include some combination of soothing one's pain, testing the loyalty and tolerance in a relationship, and/or 'hot-wiring' a new connection.

'We've only known each other for a couple of weeks, but I'm going to share this and we'll be BFFs now.'

> "Sharing our stories with people who have earned the right to hear them is the key..."

Unfortunately, for all of us who've done this (and I include myself in this group), the response is normally the opposite of what we're looking for: people recoil and shut down, compounding our shame and disconnection.

Okay, so it's obvious that there are plenty of reasons why sharing can be so difficult.

But when you do a bit of research into how incredibly powerful it is to forming deep, meaningful relationships, you should see that it's more than worth the efforts.

Brene talks a bit more about sharing and how to avoid floodlighting:

Ordinarily, when we reach out and share ourselves—our fears, hopes, struggles and joys—we create small sparks of connection.

Our shared vulnerability creates light in normally dark places.

My metaphor for this is twinkle lights. The lights are small, and a single light is not very special, but an entire strand of sparkling lights is sheer beauty.

It's the connectivity that makes them beautiful.

When it comes to vulnerability, connectivity means sharing our stories with people who have earned the right to hear them—people with whom we've cultivated relationships that can bear the weight of our story.

Sharing our stories with people who have earned the right to hear them is the key, and the part about sharing that those who 'floodlight' miss.

# Are You Asking Questions of Others That You Are Truly Interested in Knowing the Answers To?

**CURIOSITY**

## POWER PLAYER 3: CURIOSITY

**How many times do you ask people questions in your day-to-day life and really don't care about the answers?**

Before you rush in and say you always care (which is a fib), consider this question:

*"How are you?"*

We probably ask this question (or some variation of it) upwards of 20 times a day, depending on how many people we see and interact with.

Furthermore, the majority of people we ask that question are strangers or acquaintances.

You ask prospects how their day is going before you request a meeting, you ask your employees how their weekend was on a Monday morning, and you ask a host of cashiers, waitresses and gas station attendants this as you shop, eat, and fill up.

What answer do you normally hear?

*"I'm good!"*

*"Doing great!"*

*"Not bad, how about you?"*

It's very rare that you'll actually hear how these people are doing. And you know what? You probably don't really care. And that's okay.

## WHEN TO BREAK OUT OF SOCIAL NORMS

We've developed the understanding that as we go about our business, we're going to abide by social norms and ask how we are with both parties completely aware of the fact that we really aren't going to have a real conversation.

**Imagine if you did start a real conversation with every one of these people!**

You'd be stuck at the grocery store for an hour while you heard about the cashier's boyfriend cheating on her or your 10-minute phone call with a prospect would turn into a 3-hour gabfest as they shared the horrible family dinner they had to endure at their in-laws the previous evening.

While we know that social niceties keep the world spinning (and us going from one task to the next without too much distraction), the problem comes in when this lack of interest in others creeps in where it shouldn't.

It's okay to ask the cashier how her day is going without really wanting to hear a real answer, but it's something else altogether to inquire about your 9-year-old's first day of 4th grade and hope that she'll just say 'it was fine' so you can move on.

## SHOWING GENUINE INTEREST

What does being interested in someone else really boil down to? **It can be summed up in one word: curiosity.**

When we're curious about something (or someone), we try our best to learn more. We dig in deep because we find the answers interesting and we want to gain a better understanding.

And you know what's really cool? Our brains actually go through a transformation when we're curious about something.

## A STUDY ON CURIOSITY

There's an interesting study that looked at how curiosity worked in the classroom.

It basically stated that when a teacher was able to get their students curious about something, it triggered a release of the feel-good hormone dopamine in their brains.

Not only that, but as soon as the curiosity was triggered, it meant that the students retained the information they learned at a much higher rate.

But wait, there's more!!

They not only retained the information they learned on the subjects they were curious about, but they also retained more information on the boring stuff they learned before and after as well!

This article goes more in depth to the study and the implications if you're interested in hearing more.

**But the bottom line is: when we're curious about someone, it makes us feel good and we remember what they tell us.**

We're not even going into the other side of it here, which I hope is pretty obvious: when we're genuinely curious about someone else and what they're experiencing, they feel good and it's a *huge deposit* in their equity account.

Of course, the problem comes when we can't seem to muster the curiosity to get engaged.

Maybe you meet a tax accountant at a networking event and the last thing on the planet you're interested in is accounting.

Or your son comes home from a friend's house and is buzzing to tell you about the video game they played for three hours when video games are the least interesting thing in the world to you.

What do you do then?

## WHEN YOU LACK CURIOSITY

The important thing is not rushing into judging something (or someone) as boring and uninteresting to you.

Sure, maybe that tax accountant seems like a real snooze when he's talking about his business, but wait 'til you get him talking about jazz! Suddenly he's full of life and amazing stories!

Or maybe you couldn't care less about another hour-long discussion of Minecraft with your son, but if you dig a little deeper you realize that he's sharing some good stuff with you about how his friendship with his buddy is going.

When you're talking to someone you want to develop curiosity about, the best thing you can do is ask questions and listen to the answers. If they still aren't saying anything you can get excited about? **Ask more questions.**

When you're curious about someone, you're making deposits into their account while enjoying the added benefit of turning on that light in your brain that makes you feel great about life. No wonder we call it a power player!

## THE BENEFITS OF CURIOSITY

Need more encouragement to be curious? A *Harvard Business Journal* article referred to a study done on curiosity that found it to be associated with less defensive reactions to stress and less aggressive reactions to provocation.

Natural curiosity is also associated with better job performance, more open communication between team members and enhanced listening skills.

Curiosity is also one of those skills that is modeled. Want your team to be more curious and come up with innovative solutions to problems? Then *you* need to be curious.

Want your kids to think about different careers they might be interested in? They need to see *you* being curious about the world as well. Children are naturally curious from a young age (that's where all those questions come from!), but are often taught *not* to be by well-meaning parents or teachers.

So get the image of that poor cat we always reference when trying to shut down imagination. Curiosity did *not* kill it and it won't kill you. Get curious and start making deposits!

## WAYS TO FOSTER CURIOSITY

- **Hang out with other people who are curious.** The broader their interests and their desire to learn, the better!

- **Ask as many questions as you can about anything unfamiliar or confusing to you.**

- **Read outside your comfort zone.** Are you usually a novel-reader? Pick up a biography. Never read a newspaper? Now's the time to give one a try.

- **Don't shy away from the unexpected.** Last-minute invitation to a party where you won't know anyone? Go. Offered tickets to a sporting event you've never been interested in? Take them.

- **Listen without judgment.**

**THE PLATINUM RULE**

## POWER PLAYER 4: THE PLATINUM RULE

From an early age, many of us have been given the advice, "treat others as you would like to be treated."

This advice, generally known as The Golden Rule, certainly has its merits, especially when it comes to general interactions with random people.

For example, I would not want someone to yell at me and make me cry if I were a cashier at a grocery store and I could not get the scanner to work.

Therefore I should not make this poor Wal-Mart employee break down even though I'm in a hurry and all I want is to buy this Red Bull for the love of God!

There are a lot of problems with The Golden Rule.

**To illuminate, let me give you a couple of examples (that actually have happened to me).**

I had a boss who was extremely motivated by contests. This was the type of person that you could get to do nearly anything as long as there was an element of competition involved and she had a chance of beating others.

I, on the other hand, have no interest in competition and, if you pit me against someone else, I'll usually let them win if it means everyone can be happy.

Guess what she used to motivate me to make more sales? Yep, a competition between the employees. The winner got a trip.

I think you can imagine how well I did in this contest (hint: not very well, but I was sure glad my co-worker got that nifty trip!).

After a few more failed attempts at motivating me with contests, we had a talk about why this wasn't working. I told her that I didn't like competition and I'd rather just have my efforts recognized, whether they were better than the next person's or not.

Well, when the next sales cycle rolled around, she unveiled another sales contest. What does the winner get? A trip.

I'm sure you're able to guess by now how well I did (and why I continued to be a lackluster salesperson until the day I left).

**To take this to another relationship arena, I'll also give you an example of one of my good friends.**

This friend loves to talk on the phone. I, on the other hand, really don't like talking on the phone. (Okay, I kind of hate it.) I am a writer, so texting is like little writing assignments and I LOVE writing assignments.

Also, I'm a multi-tasker, so if I'm spending an hour in the evening on the phone, that is time I am not spending with my daughter, making dinner, catching up on my reading, solving the world hunger problem, etc. etc.

Well, after a few dust-ups where she expressed extreme displeasure that I rarely answered my phone or arranged 'chat dates' for us, I realized I was treating her how I liked to be treated (by texting and generally being quite blasé about whether we talked much or not).

However, on the flip side, by not returning my texts promptly (sometimes not for a day or more) and insisting we needed to talk frequently and see each other regularly to remain good friends, she was not treating me how I liked to be treated.

**So changes needed to be made by both sides.**

(On a side note, this is also a great example of how different people have different needs from their friends, as we explained in the chapter on Friendship.)

**Therein lies the problem with The Golden Rule: we are all different.**

We are motivated by different things, have different wants and needs, have different backgrounds and experiences and are in different places in our lives.

Other than very broad, general ways of being treated (no one likes to be yelled at, physically abused, insulted, etc.—and if you do, we've got some other books we can recommend), people like to be treated in ways that are very specific to them.

**We all want to feel special and we all want to know that we matter.**

When you take the time to learn from someone how they like to be treated, you are making a deposit. And then when you treat them that way? HUGE deposits.

For the people that matter most to us, it's easy to learn how they like to be treated: observe how they react to certain situations with others (and with you). If that doesn't work: ASK.

You might also want to check out *The Five Love Languages* by Gary Chapman, which is a great book about finding out how our significant others want to be shown love (there's also a follow up book for parents).

When we live our lives by The Golden Rule, we may think we're making deposits, but we actually aren't. And sometimes, such as the case with my former boss, we may actually be making withdrawals from the account because we continually ignore how a person is telling us they would like to be treated.

**We're so stuck on the thought, "This makes me happy, why isn't it making them happy, too?" that we simply forget to be curious.**

The biggest compliment we can give someone is recognizing their individuality.

As stated above, this is an easy thing to do with those closest to us if we simply pay attention. But what about with those we don't see as often, like co-workers, bosses or employees?

Author and professor Dr. Tony Alessandra has done extensive research on The Platinum Rule and has devised a way to spot four different personality types in the workplace: *the Director, Socializer, Relater and Thinker* (this can also be translated to understanding people outside of the workplace as well).

Check out his book *The Platinum Rule* to learn more about these types and how you can make deposits in their accounts.

# Using the Five Love Languages to Practice the Platinum Rule

## WORDS OF AFFIRMATION
Those with this language love to be praised and hear how you feel about them.

- **With a partner:** "I love you very much and am so proud to be your husband/wife."

- **With a co-worker:** "You did a wonderful job on that report and I could see how much the boss valued your hard work."

## PHYSICAL TOUCH
This language is all about non-verbal communication.

- **With a child:** Lots of hugs, kisses, and snuggles.

- **With a friend:** Touch their arm or shoulder when talking to them, hug hello, get them massage gift certificates for birthdays.

## RECEIVING GIFTS
Those with this language love both giving and receiving thoughtful gifts.

- **With a spouse:** Take holidays seriously when it comes to gift-giving and never miss an opportunity to bring home a little something special for no reason at all.

- **With a manager:** Bring them their favorite gourmet coffee or treat before a meeting.

## QUALITY TIME
Nothing makes those with this language happier than dedicated one-on-one time.

- **With a child:** Make sure you do things with just the two of you: go to a movie, go out to dinner or just spend some time together reading or watching a TV show.

- **With a friend:** These are high-touch friends and need to spend a lot of time with you to deepen the friendship so schedule outings or visits regularly.

## ACTS OF SERVICE
Helping out these individuals is the best way to show them you love and appreciate them.

- **With a partner:** Do some of the chores you know they hate to do without question, grumbling or insisting they do something for you in return.

- **With a co-worker:** Help them out with a report, give them a lift home or offer to pick them up something when you go to the store for lunch.

# *Effective Follow Through is the Expectation, Instead of the Norm*

**FOLLOW-THROUGH**

## POWER PLAYER 5: FOLLOW-THROUGH

I met with a potential colleague and referral partner (let's call him Stan) a few months back about a project I was working on.

Not only was this project totally in his wheelhouse, but he also asked for the meeting, telling me he really wanted to get involved.

During the meeting, Stan used numerous Engagement Equity Power Players to get me excited about his involvement.

He listened carefully to what we were doing, he asked questions, he displayed genuine curiosity, he suggested numerous ideas and contacts he could reach out to for us.

By the end of this meeting I was pumped. I came back to the office practically glowing about this meeting and what it would mean for our project.

Then I talked to my partner in the project about the great news and was crestfallen when she said, "Oh, be careful with Stan. He never does what he says he'll do."

I really couldn't believe it.

Were we talking about the same Stan?? I was so certain after our meeting that he'd be a big part of our project's success.

## WHY PEOPLE FAIL TO FOLLOW-THROUGH

But sure enough, weeks turned into months and Stan never hooked me up with the contacts he'd talked about, never showed up to meetings and slowly stopped returning my emails when I tried to check in.

What I thought was the savior of our project turned into an enormous (and frustrating) waste of my time.

Not only did I lose faith in him about keeping his word, but I also started to feel like all the Power Players he'd shown me in our meeting had been manipulative rather than genuine.

Talk about a potential great relationship going down the proverbial drain!

**Unfortunately, it seems that in our modern society, effective follow-through is the exception instead of the norm.**

Whether we're agreeing to a project that we never put any work into, telling our kids we'll be at a game and then not showing up because we're working late or ensuring our partner we'll take their pants to the dry cleaner then leaving them sitting on the bedroom floor, we as a society have a big problem with doing what we say we'll do.

*Why?*

I found a great article by a David Orman who is (of all things) a doctor of Natural Medicine. He suggests there are a number of reasons we fail to keep our word, including:

## NOT PLAYING THE MOVIE OUT IN FULL

**This means we agree to something without really thinking about how that is going to look or what a commitment it will be.**

For example, your daughter wants to take ballet lessons and you say yes, without considering how you'll pay for it, who will take her 45 minutes across town twice a week and how you or your spouse will be able to attend recitals every Saturday when you both work.

## NOT WANTING TO HURT FEELINGS

**When someone asks us to do something that we don't want to do, we somehow believe it's kinder to say yes and not do it than to say no up front.**

This is actually a pretty insensitive thing to do when we really think about it, and the initial sting of a 'no' is MUCH less damaging than the punch in the gut of not keeping your word.

## MISTAKING AN INTEREST FOR A PASSION

Interests pass and you may or may not keep the same interests (or follow up on them), while a passion is something you're committed to and will always follow up on.

When you say yes to something (or are trying to get someone else to say yes), consider which you're agreeing to. If it's a passion, be confident in that yes. If it's an interest? You might want to reconsider.

**When we follow through on something, no matter how large or small, we are building trust (and making deposits).**

When you tell your new colleague you'll introduce him to your Realtor friend and you send that email or make that call the next day... DEPOSIT

When you tell your daughter you'll take her out to your favorite restaurant the next evening because she got all As and you leave work early to ensure you can get a table... DEPOSIT

When your friend makes a plan to see a concert with you and you turn down other invitations to make sure you're able to go... DEPOSIT

Like most of the other Engagement Power Players we talk about, if you slip up every once in a while, it's not going to have a huge impact on the relationship. We're all human and we can't do everything perfectly every time. However, if you're making enough deposits, you have earned the right to ask for a little understanding (WITHDRAWAL) when you flub.

When you have a consistent history, you build trust. Your business associates, friends and family come to think of you as someone they can count on, and your relationships get deeper and more gratifying.

**THE ASK**

## POWER PLAYER 6: THE ASK

I write blogs for a video production company. Because this arrangement got going right when we first formed our business, we cut a little deal with them that I would write their blogs in exchange for them doing a video or two for our business down the line.

It was agreed upon that I would build up some credit (equity!) by writing a few blogs, then would in turn ask them for a video when it made sense (WITHDRAWAL).

Wow, even back then Engagement Equity was in play and I didn't even realize it.

Well, as time went on, their blogs became more and more of a regular thing. Invariably, I would spend some time Monday morning focused on their blog work and get it uploaded to their site before I continued on with my day.

It wasn't a big deal in my mind.

I enjoyed the work, it was easy and I didn't put much thought into the fact that I wasn't being paid for it.

Every once in a while, I'd get an inquiry from them asking if I'd decided what I'd like my video to be on.

## GIVING WITHOUT AN ASK

Well, I could never quite decide if we wanted to focus on the marketing side of our business or if I'd rather save it for one of our special projects.

So I kept pushing them off, assuring them I'd let them know when the time was right.

You'd think they'd be pretty happy about this arrangement, right? I mean, they had a relationship with someone who was continuing to make deposits into their equity account without ever asking for a withdrawal!

Who could ask for anything better? Well, as you can imagine, that's not at all how they felt.

The questions started to get more urgent.

*"When can we meet to talk about your video?"*

*"Let's get a pre-production video meeting scheduled, Angela!"*

*"Happy Friday! Just a reminder that we need to talk about your video! Have a great weekend."*

The last one was my favorite because I started to get it EVERY FRIDAY. These people were serious! They wanted a withdrawal and they wanted it now!

The reason I relate this story is because it illustrates how important 'the ask' or the 'withdrawal' is to the Engagement Equity equation.

If you're like most people, this is probably the sticking point to the whole ball of wax. A lot of you don't mind giving value to others. In fact, you enjoy helping out and get a warm fuzzy feeling when you know you've done something that's helped make another person's life better.

But if you're that type of person, you probably also have a tough time asking for things in return. It seems selfish. And this whole 'giving 3-4 times for every time you take' idea seems manipulative.

## IT IS OKAY TO ASK

Just like in my previous example, most people want to believe they've got a pretty equal relationship going with most people in their lives.

> "Because there was no 'ask', all the value of their deposits had been negated."

Whether it's a business relationship or personal, no one likes to feel that they are taking a whole lot more than they're giving (or vice versa).

Did you ever have one of those friends who was so desperate to be liked that they would do anything for you?

This is the friend who would get a new CD and when you said you liked that band, they'd give it to you before it was even opened (going back to the olden days of CDs here!). The same friend who would always trade lunches with you even though you had a crappy PB&J and they had a chicken salad on a croissant with homemade cookies and a designer soda. They'd walk your dog and do your homework and tell you you were pretty and never ask for a damn thing in return.

More than likely, if you had this person in your life, he or she wasn't your best friend. In fact, you probably didn't even really consider them a 'friend' at all. Why? Because there was no equality.

They were a pushover and a doormat. The equity account between you got so heavily weighted on one side that the relationship never had a chance to flourish.

**Because there was no 'ask', all the value of their deposits had been negated.**

And this is what I realized I had been doing with my colleague. I put a lot of work into those blogs. They were good (and I knew the video company recognized that). But they were starting to get very uncomfortable with the unbalanced nature of our relationship and, if I pushed it back much longer, my work would start to lose its value.

# With No 'Ask' the Value of Deposits Are Negated

I would become the doormat friend from high school who was always giving them my gourmet lunches and telling them they looked pretty!!

Never being one to trade my gourmet lunches for anything, you can bet I got that video pre-production meeting scheduled!

**The moral of this story is: the withdrawal is just as important as the deposits.**

One does not work without the other.

And while the depositing can get to be really fun (especially once you realize how easy it is to make deposits with our other Power Players like Listening and Curiosity), it's likely that the withdrawal will continue to be the difficult part to put into practice.

Our advice? Keep practicing. Once you see that a well-timed ask can be just as fulfilling as making deposits, you'll get better and better at it.

## TIPS ON MAKING ASKS

- **Always be respectful.** Even if you think you 'deserve' whatever you're asking for, there's never an excuse to be rude or demanding.

- **Keep timing in mind.** Making an ask when the other person is stressed, overwhelmed, or busy with another project is not likely to go over well.

- **Be specific.** *"Hey, can I get some referrals from you some time?"* is not specific. *"Can we sit down next week and go over your client list to identify*

*one or two who might benefit from my services?"* is much better.

- **Follow up.** Your ask may not be received and acted on right away. Follow up a few days after making it to see if there is any more information you need to provide.

- **Make your ask in person.** If you're uncomfortable asking for things, you might try to get away with sending a text or email with your ask. However, you're much more likely to be successful if you do so in person and create a conversation around the ask. This also deepens your relationship with the person you're asking.

- **Make sure the ask matches how much equity you've earned.** Making a huge ask from whom you've only built up a small amount of equity is a recipe for disaster. While it's okay to make little asks of someone you have a lot of equity with, the opposite is not recommended.

- **Be ready to explain.** While some people are comfortable saying yes to asks they don't really understand, many are not. Even if you've built up plenty of equity for the ask, you may still need to further describe the project you need a donation for, etc. Understand this doesn't mean you won't get a 'yes,' just that more information is required.

# Recognize When It's Necessary to Close The Account

**CLOSING THE ACCOUNT**

## POWER PLAYER 7: CLOSING THE ACCOUNT

It may not seem like a 'power player', but knowing when enough is enough and closing the account you share with someone is an incredibly important part of the Engagement Equity strategy.

Why?

Because if you don't know where to draw the line, you'll inevitably get taken advantage of too many times, you'll lose your passion for engagement and go back to the 'what have you done for me lately?' mindset.

There are a number of situations where closing the account is the best option and sometimes it has absolutely nothing to do with the other person being a 'taker' or an otherwise negative individual.

It's important to keep in mind that even if you do have to close the account with someone, it does not need to turn into bitterness or a relationship that is now marked by animosity.

**It simply means that, for whatever reason, you are no longer making deposits into this account until the circumstances or situation changes.**

91

## IT'S OKAY TO CLOSE AN ACCOUNT

Just like with a benevolent bank, you always have the option of re-opening the account if the time comes when it makes sense to do so.

As you get more and more into the Engagement Equity way of life, you'll see that some account closings are more painful and difficult than others.

While it may be relatively easy to see that the sales prospect you've been pursuing is never going to become a client and therefore you need to spend your energy (and deposits) elsewhere, it's much more difficult to make this determination with a friend or a romantic partner.

The more emotions involved in a relationship, the more difficult it will be to close the account.

However, these may be the most important ones to make that decision with. Why?

Because if they are that emotionally involved and if you are constantly making deposits with no reciprocation, they're putting an enormous strain on you.

If you keep enough of these accounts open, you'll have no energy left for the people who want to build their accounts with you and it could hamper your ability to radiate outward.

## THE RIGHT TIME TO CLOSE AN ACCOUNT

I wish I could boil it down to a simple ratio, such as: if you've made 15 subsequent deposits into your shared account and have not been able to make a single withdrawal, it's time to close up shop.

Unfortunately, it's not that easy.

Every relationship (and therefore every account) has its own unique story, energy and effect on your life. While it may not take much to keep an account open in one area of your life, it may be emotionally devastating to keep an account open in another.

So, how do you know it's time to close an account?

**When it becomes a burden that is taking away from other relationships in that area of your life.**

Only you can determine when a relationship reaches this status, and some people have a much higher tolerance for relationships that take a lot of work than others do.

Closing an account is not only a relief and a lightening of a load that you no longer need to carry, but it also sets a standard. It shows people how much you will stand for and what you're willing to put up with to keep a relationship going.

**Whether you know it or not, you're telling people every single day how you'll accept being treated.**

You may TELL people how you WANT to be treated, but what they're really paying attention to (and acting on) is how you're SHOWING them you'll allow yourself to be treated.

## RESTORING RELATIONSHIPS

Do you have relationships in your life that make your stomach twist and turn when you think about them?

Do you find yourself constantly arguing with or having to make concessions for a couple of people in your life?

Is it because you haven't been focused on making deposits or is it because you've been making too many deposits and getting nothing in return?

Now is a good time to re-evaluate these relationships and determine if you need to change how you interact with the other person or if it's just time to let the relationship go.

# Conclusion

I hope you've enjoyed Engagement Equity and learned a little about how to strengthen relationships and add value to your life and to the lives of others.

When you start putting this into practice, I think you'll be amazed at the transformation in your life in both your personal and professional areas.

Though it may be difficult at first to focus on making frequent deposits—especially if you feel you aren't getting a lot in return—I guarantee it will pay off in the long run.

Thank you for reading our book and please follow our company, Pixel Fire Marketing, on social media. We promise to make lots of deposits in our shared account!

**@ANGELAWOLTMAN**

**Angela Woltman**

# About Pixel Fire Marketing

Pixel Fire Marketing is a full-service online marketing agency based in Omaha, NE.

The company, which is owned by Dan DeSive, Raina Garcia and Angela Chaney, specializes in website design, social media marketing, content strategy and lead generation.

Pixel Fire's strategy across platforms is based on the Engagement Equity concept and they wholeheartedly believe that this philosophy is the secret to success in marketing, business and life.

**Book Design & Layout:** Taysia Peterson | **Engagement Equity Branding:** Sarah Nelson

**f** @PIXELFIREMKTG          **O** @PIXELFIREMKTG          **y** @PIXELFIREMKTG

www.ingramcontent.com/pod-product-compliance
Lightning Source LLC
Chambersburg PA
CBHW040929210326
41597CB00030B/5233